NEIL ARMSTRONG
FIRST MAN ON THE MOON

Neil Armstrong

Jackie Robinson

Harriet Tubman

Jane Goodall

»TRAIL BLAZERS
NEIL ARMSTRONG
FIRST MAN ON THE MOON

ALEX WOOLF

RANDOM HOUSE 🏠 NEW YORK

Text copyright © 2019 by Alex Woolf
Cover art copyright © 2019 by Luisa Uribe and George Ermos
Interior illustrations copyright © 2019 by Artful Doodlers
Trailblazers logo design by Mike Burroughs

All rights reserved. Published in the United States by Random House Children's Books, a division of Penguin Random House LLC, New York.

Random House and the colophon are registered trademarks of Penguin Random House LLC.

Visit us on the Web! rhcbooks.com

Educators and librarians, for a variety of teaching tools, visit us at RHTeachersLibrarians.com

Library of Congress Cataloging-in-Publication Data
Name: Woolf, Alex, author.
Title: Neil Armstrong: first man on the moon / Alex Woolf.
Description: First edition. | New York: Random House, 2019. | Series: Trailblazers |
Audience: Ages 8 to 12. | Includes bibliographical references and index.
Identifiers: LCCN 2019009145 (print) | LCCN 2019011483 (ebook) | ISBN 978-0-593-12401-7 (trade pbk.) | ISBN 978-0-593-12402-4 (lib. bdg.) | ISBN 978-0-593-12403-1 (ebook)
Subjects: LCSH: Armstrong, Neil, 1930–2012—Juvenile literature. | Project Apollo (U.S.)—Juvenile literature. | Astronauts—United States—Biography—Juvenile literature. | Space flight to the moon—History—Juvenile literature.
Classification: LCC TL789.85.A75 (ebook) | LCC TL789.85.A75 W66 2019 (print) | DDC 629.450092 [B]—dc23

Created by Stripes Publishing Limited, an imprint of the Little Tiger Group

Printed in the United States of America
10 9 8 7 6 5 4 3 2 1

First Edition

Random House Children's Books supports the First Amendment and celebrates the right to read.

Contents

Introduction
One Small Step — **1**

Chapter 1
Small-Town Boy — **13**

Chapter 2
Learning to Fly — **31**

Chapter 3
The Heat of Battle — **49**

Chapter 4
To the Limits — **67**

Chapter 5
Journey into Space — **83**

Chapter 6
One Giant Leap — **101**

Chapter 7
Reluctant Hero — **121**

Conclusion
Inspiring Others — **139**

Timeline — **152**

Further Reading — **156**

Glossary — **158**

Index — **162**

One Sunday evening, 238,855 miles (384,400 km) above Earth, an astronaut crawled through the hatch of *Apollo 11*'s lunar module (LM). Neil Armstrong, dressed in his bulky spacesuit, began descending the ladder toward the silver surface beneath him. A television camera attached to the spacecraft sent blurry black-and-white images of his progress to hundreds of millions of people watching back on Earth.

It was July 20, 1969, one of the most important dates in the history of exploration. For the first time, a human being was going to set foot on the moon.

"The surface appears to be very, very fine-grained as you get close to it," Neil reported. "It's almost like a powder."

He continued down the ladder until he reached the bottommost rung. "I'm going to step off the LM now," he said. None of the millions of people watching on their television sets would ever forget the next moment as, very slowly, he stepped off the ladder and planted his left foot on lunar soil.

THE SPACE RACE

So why was Neil Armstrong on the moon in the first place? Well, it was all because of a competition that had started when he was a teenager—a competition not between people, but between countries.

After World War II ended in 1945, the world was dominated by two great powers—the United States and the Soviet Union—and they began a rivalry known as the Cold War. Both countries recruited German rocket scientists who had worked on long-range missiles during the war to help them build a new generation of rockets. These missiles were armed with nuclear warheads and could reach the enemy across a distance of thousands of miles. Rockets with such power also had the potential to launch a satellite into orbit, and the two nations soon began to compete for the conquest of space. It became known as the:

SPACE RACE

The Soviet Union got off to a great start. On October 4, 1957, they launched Earth's first artificial satellite, Sputnik 1. This was followed in November of that year by Sputnik 2, which carried the first animal, a dog named Laika, into orbit.

LAIKA

The Americans were shocked into action. They sped up their own program, and in December 1957 invited the world's press to observe the launch of their first satellite. Unfortunately, the Vanguard rocket exploded on the launchpad.

They should have called it Kaputnik.

This was a national humiliation, and the Americans realized they had work to do to catch up with the Soviet Union. The following month, they successfully launched their first satellite, Explorer 1, and in July 1958, the United States established a new organization called the National Aeronautics and Space Administration (NASA), which was dedicated to advancing space exploration. Meanwhile, the Soviets kept piling up more achievements:

January 4, 1959

LUNA 1 FIRST SPACECRAFT TO TRAVEL CLOSE TO MOON

SEPTEMBER 14, 1

LUNA 2 STRIKES MOON'S SURFACE!

April 12, 1961

OVIET PILOT YURI GAGARIN ECOMES FIRST HUMAN IN SPACE!

May 19, 1961

VENERA 1 FLIES BY VENUS

June 16, 1963

ALENTINA TERESHKOVA: FIRST WOMAN IN SPACE

⋛ MAN ON THE MOON ⋚

In December 1958, NASA announced a space program called Project Mercury. They began launching their own astronauts into space, starting with Alan Shepard in May 1961. Yet the Americans knew they would have to come up with something much more ambitious if they were ever to gain a lead in the Space Race. On May 25, 1961, US President John F. Kennedy set out a new objective:

I believe that this nation should commit itself to achieving the goal, before this decade is out, of landing a man on the moon and returning him safely to Earth.

The idea of landing a man on the moon in just eight years seemed wildly optimistic in 1961, considering how little America had achieved in space until that point. But the government poured billions of dollars into the project. Mercury was followed by Project Gemini, which aimed to develop space-travel techniques to support a moon landing.

SATURN V

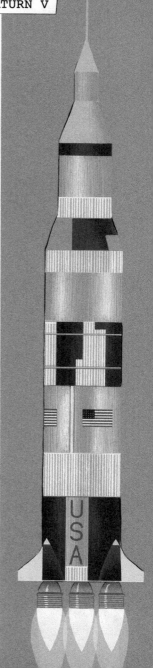

Between March 1965 and November 1966, ten crewed Gemini missions flew, and some remarkable advances were made. Astronauts took the first spacewalks—stepping outside their craft in spacesuits. They also learned how to join two spacecraft in orbit, which is called docking. These were all crucial steps on the road to the moon landing.

Gemini was followed by the Apollo program. The Apollo spacecraft were the first to take astronauts beyond Earth orbit to the moon. They were carried into orbit by a rocket called Saturn V. Taller than the Statue of Liberty, the Saturn V was the biggest, heaviest, and most powerful rocket in history. The spacecraft included a command/service module, carrying the crew and supplies, and the lunar module for landing on the moon.

Apollo 1 Tragedy

The Apollo program began with a tragedy. On January 27, 1967, during a preflight test for Apollo 1, a spark lit the pure oxygen inside the command module. The spacecraft burst into flames, and the three astronauts inside—Gus Grissom, Ed White, and Roger Chaffee—were killed. After a delay to establish the cause of the accident and make safety improvements, NASA resumed the program.

In December 1968, *Apollo 8* became the first spacecraft to take humans beyond Earth orbit. Astronauts James Lovell, Frank Borman, and William "Bill" Anders were the very first people to see Earth as a planet. They went into orbit around the moon and saw the moon's far side, which is never visible from Earth.

The Apollo 10 mission involved practicing docking the lunar module with the command/service module in lunar orbit. By now, astronauts had practiced almost everything and had proven it to work. Neil Armstrong would command the next mission, Apollo 11. It aimed to land a man on the moon.

Famous First Words

So many thousands of people had been involved over a great many years in the project to send a man to the moon. There had been moments of inspiration, exhilaration, frustration, danger, and sacrifice. When Neil Armstrong stepped out onto the moon on July 20, 1969, his first words summed up the immensity of this collective achievement:

"That's one small step for [a] man, one giant leap for mankind."

CHAPTER 1
SMALL-TOWN BOY

Neil Alden Armstrong was born on August 5, 1930, in a farmhouse belonging to his grandparents in rural Ohio. For a boy who grew up wanting only to fly, his parents chose a good name for him, as *Neil* comes from the Gaelic *Néall*, which many have interpreted to mean *cloud*.

I was born and raised in Ohio, about sixty miles north of Dayton.

Dayton was the home of the Wright brothers, the inventors of powered flight. They were among Neil's earliest heroes, and their invention, in more ways than one, would come to dominate his life.

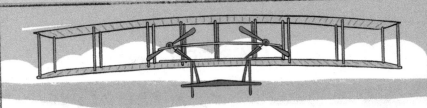

The Wright Brothers

Orville and Wilbur Wright were engineers and inventors from Dayton, Ohio. In 1903, they did something extraordinary: they built the first airplane powered by an engine, rather than one that glided on the wind. Their one-seater plane, the Wright Flyer, was made of wood and cloth. It made its first successful flight on December 17, 1903, at Kitty Hawk, North Carolina. The flight lasted just twelve seconds!

Neil's parents were Stephen and Viola Armstrong. Stephen worked as an auditor for the Ohio state government. This job required him to move from place to place on quite a regular basis; as a result, the family lived in sixteen different small towns during the first fourteen years of Neil's life. This did not seem to faze Neil, as he always managed to adapt to his new home, and he made friends easily. Even so, his closest companions growing up were undoubtedly his sister and brother: June came along in July 1933, and Dean followed in February 1935.

THE TIN GOOSE

Neil's love of airplanes started very early. When he was just two years old, his father took him to watch the Cleveland Air Races. Neil was so impressed that he persuaded his parents to buy him a toy airplane. Soon he was zooming around the house with it! About four years later, Neil experienced his first real airplane flight. By this time, the family had moved to a town called Warren. One Sunday in July 1936, not long before Neil's sixth birthday, Stephen took Neil to the local airfield. Stephen had heard that a pilot was offering plane rides for just twenty-five cents.

Aircraft Fact File

Name:	Ford Tri-Motor
Nickname:	"Tin Goose"
Type:	High-wing monoplane
Length:	49 ft. 10 in. (15.2 m)
Wingspan:	74 ft. (22.6 m)
Passenger capacity:	12
Cruising speed:	120 mph (193 kmh)

The plane was nicknamed the "Tin Goose," because it looked as if it were made of tin (it was actually aluminum) and was shaped a bit like a big goose. Neil and his dad took their seats, and the engine rattled and roared as the plane took off. Stephen later admitted he had been scared to death. Neil, however, loved every minute!

From that day forward, aircraft became the focus of Neil's life. He read popular magazines about airplanes, cutting out his favorite pictures and sticking them in a scrapbook. He soon became an expert at identifying different kinds of aircraft. At age eight or nine, when he was living in St. Marys, Ohio, he began to build model airplanes. At first, he built them from kits. Later, he designed his own out of balsa wood, glue, and tissue paper. He hung the ones he was proudest of from his bedroom ceiling. Others he would launch from an upstairs window by means of a twisted rubber band, sometimes after setting fire to them!

Around this time, Neil challenged himself to climb the biggest tree in the backyard of their St. Marys home, a tall silver maple. This may have been an early attempt by Neil to explore what it felt like to fly, or at least get high above the ground! When he'd ascended to around fifteen feet, he mistook a dead branch for a solid one and plummeted, landing flat on his back. "Should I get Mama?" asked June, worried by the sight of her brother looking so pale and still. Neil shook his head, then changed his mind. "Yeah," he said weakly, and June ran yelling to the house. Luckily, Neil wasn't badly hurt.

Heavy fog over the Atlantic made navigating difficult for Lindbergh.

Charles Lindbergh

When Neil was young, airplanes were still seen as unusual and exciting. Just three years before Neil was born, in 1927, Charles Lindbergh had become the first person to fly solo, nonstop, across the Atlantic. Lindbergh set out from Long Island on May 20 in a small, single-engine plane called *Spirit of St. Louis*. He had no radio or parachute. Thirty-three and a half hours later, he landed in Paris. A crowd of 100,000 had gathered there to greet him. Overnight, Lindbergh became the most famous man in the world, much like Neil would just over forty years later.

⋛ BOOKS AND PLANES ⋚

Neil's mother, Viola, read to him as often as she could, instilling in him a deep and lifelong love of books. By age three, Neil could read street signs, and during his first year in elementary school, he read over a hundred books! When he got to second grade, Neil was already reading books aimed at fourth-grade pupils. The school moved him up a grade, and he still managed to get top marks. He achieved all of this in spite of having to move regularly to different towns and schools.

Neil's favorite books were, unsurprisingly, about airplanes and flying. He especially loved to read about early aviators:

→ Louis Blériot, who made the first airplane flight across the English Channel, in July 1909

→ John Alcock and Arthur Brown, who made the first nonstop transatlantic flight, in June 1919

→ Wiley Post and Harold Gatty, who were the first to fly around the world, in June/July 1931

→ Amelia Earhart, who became the first woman to fly solo across the Atlantic, in May 1932

Later in life, as Neil embarked on his own career as an aviator, he regretted that he had been born one generation too late and had missed out on those pioneering days and record-setting flights across the oceans. Little did he know then that he would one day make a flight as historic as any of his boyhood heroes!

KOTCHO, BUD, AND THE WOLF PATROL

Perhaps Neil's happiest time during his childhood was spent in the town of Upper Sandusky. The Armstrongs moved there when Neil was eleven, and he quickly settled in. His best friends from school were Konstantin "Kotcho" Solacoff and John "Bud" Blackford. Kotcho could be a prankster. Once, when they were in the chemistry lab at school, he handed Neil a dish containing some white grains and dared Neil to try some.

To afford materials for his model airplanes and magazines, Neil needed to earn some money. His first job was mowing the lawn at the local cemetery for ten cents an hour. After that, he worked at Neumeister's Bakery. He started work each day at four in the afternoon and wouldn't get off until nine or ten at night. Neil stacked the fresh loaves on the shelves and baked the doughnuts—110 each night! Because he was small for his age, Neil was the one who had to crawl inside the giant dough-mixing vats and scrape them clean. The biggest bonus of his job at Neumeister's was that he got to eat the leftover ice cream and homemade chocolates!

On December 7, 1941, just a few months after Neil's arrival in Upper Sandusky, an event occurred that shook the nation. Neil was playing in the front yard when his father called him in to listen to the news being announced on the radio. The Japanese had just launched a devastating attack on the US fleet at Pearl Harbor in Hawaii.

The following day, the US Congress declared war on Japan. News of the war filled the airwaves and newspapers, and became the major topic of conversation. For Neil, life continued much as before, but he couldn't help noticing the changes. Young men—some of them the older brothers of his friends—were drafted into the armed forces, and their families proudly displayed a star in their front windows.

Upper Sandusky didn't have a Boy Scout troop at the time the Armstrongs moved there. But in response to the war, Ohio's Boy Scout Troop 25 was established, and they met once a month in a large hall above a bank. Neil, Kotcho, Bud, and some other boys formed a unit within the troop called the Wolf Patrol. Neil was appointed the patrol scribe.

The Wolf Patrol met every week at each other's houses and worked on gaining their Tenderfoot Scout badge. Part of this involved going on hikes and learning to make and use maps. They even went camping one night in the woods by the Sandusky River, where they built a campfire and cooked on it.

Kotcho and Bud shared Neil's hobby of building model airplanes, and one of the activities of the Wolf Patrol was making models of fighter and bomber aircraft. In a small way this helped the war effort, because the scout leaders sent these models to military and civil defense authorities to help them distinguish between Allied and enemy aircraft.

Scouts in Space

Out of 294 people who became astronauts from 1959 through 2003, more than 200 had been in the Scouts, including 21 women who were former Girl Scouts. And of the 12 men to walk on the moon, 11 had been active in scouting.

SCHOOL DAYS

Neil was becoming very busy. As well as school, he had his job at Neumeister's Bakery and his weekly meetings with the Wolf Patrol.

Once they had attained Tenderfoot rank in the Scouts, Neil, Kotcho, and Bud immediately began working for their Eagle Scout badge. They had to undertake a twenty-mile (32-km) hike in a single day. So early one morning, they set out for Carey, Ohio, which lay ten miles (16 km) to the north. When they reached Carey, they ate lunch at a restaurant converted from an old windmill. On the return journey, the boys grew tired and their pace slowed. Neil started to worry that he was going to be late for his job at Neumeister's Bakery, which started at 4 p.m. According to Kotcho, "Fatigue was setting in. . . . Neil kept pushing us to go faster and faster so he could get to work. We told him to go ahead." So Neil adopted the "Boy Scouts pace" to get home faster. This involved alternately running and walking, switching each time he reached a roadside telephone pole. His efforts paid off, and he made it to the bakery on time.

Neil and Bud also played in the school orchestra. Neil had enjoyed music from a very young age, when his mother, Viola, taught him to play the piano. Despite his small size, Neil chose to play one of the biggest instruments in the school orchestra, the baritone horn. It was a sort of cross between a trumpet and a trombone. When Viola asked him why he had opted for such a big instrument, Neil replied that he liked the tone. Some evenings, the family gathered to play music together, with Viola on piano, Neil on horn, June on violin, and Dean on cornet.

Kotcho, Neil, and Bud liked school, especially science, and they competed with each other to get the best grades. The three of them decided to enter a project for the Bowling Green State University Science Fair. Bud and Kotcho planned to build a photoelectric cell. They would shine a light on the cell and produce electricity.

Neil wanted to work on his own project: a steam turbine made out of wood. He cut up some wood and glued it together to make a frame to which he attached a little wheel. Then, he filled a small pan with water and heated it with a candle. The steam rising from the pan caused the wheel to rotate. Meanwhile, Kotcho and Bud were struggling to get their photoelectric cell to work. On the eve of the science fair, they abandoned the project. Instead, they hastily put together a pinhole camera using an oatmeal box covered with tissue paper.

The next day at the science fair, Neil proudly showed off his steam turbine to visitors, refilling the pan with water several times, as it kept boiling away. Just before the judges arrived, Neil heated the water, then blew out the candle. When the judges approached, he relit it. The steam rose, but for some reason the wheel didn't turn! The judges waited patiently for a moment before moving on.

Neil discovered later that he'd run the turbine so much that morning, the wood surrounding the wheel had swollen with moisture, stopping it from turning. In the end, Kotcho and Bud won first prize for a project they had thrown together at the last minute!

CHAPTER 2
LEARNING TO FLY

When Neil was fourteen, the family moved to Wapakoneta, in western Ohio. Although Neil was sad to say goodbye to his friends in Upper Sandusky, he felt reasonably at home in Wapakoneta. His grandparents' farmhouse, which he visited regularly, was just six miles (ten km) from the town. The Armstrongs bought a large two-story corner house, and Neil soon filled his new bedroom with his model airplanes.

He attended Blume High School, which was only a few blocks from his house. It was a small, friendly school with just four hundred pupils. Neil quickly settled in. He joined the school orchestra and the boys' glee club. He also became active in the local Boy Scout troop. Like the old Wolf Patrol, his new patrol met weekly to work on their merit badges.

Neil was maturing into a quiet and thoughtful young man. His new friends didn't think of him as shy, exactly, but as "a person of few words" who "thought before he spoke." One friend, Ned Keiber, said, "He just had things to do and he did them and he didn't talk about it." Sometimes Neil showed his fun side, though. After a football game, the high school band did a parade downtown. His friend Jerre Maxson remembered:

> "Neil would turn his cap around and march backward, just for laughs."

THE MISSISSIPPI MOONSHINERS

Neil's best friends at Blume were Bob Gustafson, Jerre Maxson, and Jim Mougey. Like Neil, they all enjoyed music, and the four of them decided to form a jazz combo to perform at a school assembly. Neil, of course, was on baritone horn; Jerre and Bob both played trombone; and Jim played clarinet. They called themselves the Mississippi Moonshiners. After a successful turn at the school assembly, they were booked to play at the school dance.

Blume High School Dance
Featuring
THE MISSISSIPPI MOONSHINERS
Free Admission
Saturday, June 21, 1947 · 6:30 p.m. to 9:30 p.m.

As they improved, they were even invited to play gigs at local venues. One time, they played two nights at a couple of dance halls in nearby Uniopolis and Saint Johns. This earned them a grand total of five dollars, which they had to split four ways. Of Neil's playing, Jerre recalled, "Neil was a very good musician. He had a strong driving afterbeat, you know, and really kept us going." Bob wasn't quite so kind: "Neil only knew one song by heart," he laughed, and that was the "'Flight of the Bumblebee.' . . . I can still hear that one today!" As for Neil, he thought music could help him focus, and he always tried to improve his playing, but he never thought the Moonshiners would make much money.

⋛ FLYING LESSONS ⋚

Airplanes remained Neil's first love. His dream was to become both a pilot and an aeronautical engineer—someone who designs and builds planes. About three or four miles outside Wapakoneta was Port Koneta Airport. Neil cycled or hitchhiked there as often as he could to watch the planes land and take off, and talk to the pilots.

When he was fifteen, Neil began saving up for flying lessons. He got a job at Rhine and Brading's Pharmacy, where he earned forty cents an hour. A one-hour flying lesson cost nine dollars, so he had to work twenty-two and a half hours to pay for one lesson! Neil supplemented his earnings at the pharmacy by offering to wash down the airplanes at Port Koneta. He even helped the airport mechanics with some routine maintenance work, servicing the planes' cylinders, pistons, and valves.

Eventually, Neil had saved up enough money to pay for some lessons. A veteran army pilot named Aubrey Knudegard taught him. They flew in a light, high-wing monoplane called an Aeronca Champion.

Aircraft Fact File

Name:	Aeronca Champion
Nickname:	"Champ"
Length:	21.5 ft. (6.6 m)
Wingspan:	35.2 ft. (10.7 m)
Engine:	65 horsepower
Top speed:	100 mph (161 kmh)
First flight:	April 29, 1944

Throughout the summer of 1946, Neil learned the basics of taking off, landing, and controlling and maneuvering an airplane in flight.

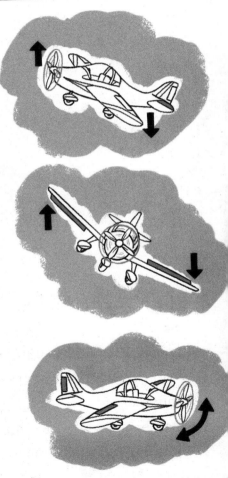

(1) The **elevators** make the plane's nose go up and down. They control the **pitch**.

(2) The **ailerons** raise and lower the wings. They control the plane's **roll**.

(3) The **rudder** and the **ailerons** work together to make the plane's nose turn left or right. They control the **yaw**.

On August 5, his sixteenth birthday, Neil received his student pilot's license. A week or two later, he made his first solo flight. He didn't expect it to happen so soon, and didn't even have a chance to alert his family and friends so they could come and watch. One day, Aubrey Knudegard had just decided Neil was ready.

Neil's brother, Dean, who helped mow the grass at the airfield, happened to be there to witness the event. He watched Neil make a couple of successful takeoffs and landings before bringing the plane back to the hangar.

Neil's parents, Viola and Stephen, were proud of their son's achievement, but Viola was too nervous to watch him fly. The dangers of aviation were brought home to all of them one Saturday afternoon about a year later. On July 26, 1947, Stephen was driving Neil and Dean back from Boy Scout camp when they saw a small plane strike a power line and crash into a hayfield. Stephen pulled the car over, and the three of them jumped a fence and raced over to the wrecked Aeronca Champion. They tried to administer first aid to the plane's two occupants. One of the men, a flying instructor, survived. Sadly, his student, twenty-year-old Carl Lange, died.

Neil was shaken by the incident and spent most of the next two days in his room by himself. It didn't put him off flying, however. By this time Neil had already completed two long-distance solo flights, making a grand total of 515 miles (829 km) in the air, and he was gaining confidence all the time.

GOING TO COLLEGE

Neil studied hard at school, especially in math and science. He knew he needed good grades in these subjects if he was to earn a place at college to study aeronautical engineering (AE). He heard that the US Navy was offering college scholarships. Although he wasn't really interested in a naval career, he thought it was worth applying, because it could pay for his college fees. In the spring of his senior year, Neil received a letter.

COMMANDER
NAVY RECRUITING COMMAND

Dear Neil,

I take great pleasure in offering you a four-year scholarship through enrollment in the 1948 US Naval Aviation College Program.

The program requires a commitment from you of seven years: two years of study at any school accredited by the navy, followed by three years of service, after which you will be able to complete your final two years of college.

This offer demonstrates our country's faith in your ability to carry out your responsibilities as a prospective officer of the United States Navy.

This was fantastic news because only a month earlier, he had been offered a place at Purdue University in West Lafayette, Indiana, to study aeronautical engineering. The navy's offer meant he could afford to go there. It seemed like his dreams were coming true!

Neil began at Purdue University shortly after his seventeenth birthday in September 1947. He enjoyed the coursework very much, because it didn't just teach him the theory of AE, but also the practical skills of building aircraft. Students had three hours of classes each morning, followed by three hours of lab work each afternoon. In his first semester, Neil learned how to weld, machine, and heat-treat metals, and do sand-casting.

When he wasn't studying, Neil pursued his other hobbies, including playing his baritone horn in the university orchestra. He also continued to build model aircraft. Not content with just building them, he also began fitting them with gasoline engines and flying them. He joined the Aeromodelers Club at Purdue and entered his planes in a number of competitions. The models were connected to the operator by wires called "control lines" and reached speeds well over 100 miles (160 km) per hour. At first Neil wasn't very successful, as this letter to his family shows:

> Today, we went to Indianapolis to the first model airplane contest. My control lines broke on the first official flight so I didn't have a chance to win anything.

But with hard work and determination, he went on to win or place second in a number of these events.

⋛ NEIL GETS HIS WINGS ⋛

In the autumn of 1948, the navy told Neil that he would begin his military service early, after just four semesters at Purdue, rather than two years. So in February 1949, he reported for navy flight training at a naval base in Pensacola, Florida. After passing his medical exams, he pledged an oath as a midshipman, the lowest grade of naval officer. For the next sixteen weeks, Neil and his fellow midshipmen did their preflight training. They studied:

- → aerial navigation
- → communications
- → engineering
- → aerology (study of the atmosphere and weather forecasting)
- → principles of flight

They also completed eighty-seven hours of intensive physical training, including a mile-long swim in the base's pool. In one exercise, known as the "Dilbert Dunker," the candidate was strapped fully clothed into a replica of a cockpit. The cockpit, on a set of rails, was sent hurtling into a deep swimming pool. The candidate had to unbuckle themselves, open the canopy, escape the cockpit, and swim to the surface before running out of breath.

Several of the candidates required assistance, but Neil managed it without difficulty.

They completed their preflight training in June 1948, and Neil did well, finishing near the top 10 percent of his class. Now they were ready to move on to the first stage of flight training. Neil got to fly an SNJ, which was a combat aircraft used to train pilots in World War II. He found the SNJ, with its 600-horsepower engine, a big step up from the little Champ he flew back in Wapakoneta.

Aircraft Fact File

Name:	North American SNJ
Also known as:	North American T6 Texan
Purpose:	Training military pilots
Length:	29 ft. (8.8 m)
Wingspan:	42 ft. (12.8 m)
Top speed:	208 mph (335 kmh)
Rate of climb:	1,200 ft./min. (6.1 m/s)

Neil trained hard in the SNJ, especially on his landings, which he struggled with. On September 7, a month after he'd turned eighteen, he made his first navy solo flight. Afterward, to celebrate this achievement, Neil's friends cut off the lower half of his tie—an old naval tradition.

Soon, Neil learned aerobatics—loops, rolls, and other flying maneuvers. He learned "partial panel" flying, when his instructors would turn off one of the instruments, such as the altimeter (the height indicator) or the gyroscopic horizon (an instrument showing the plane's orientation compared to Earth's horizon). Neil then had to fly using the other instruments along with visual clues observed through the cockpit window. He made a couple of night flights, and learned formation flying, ground strafing, and dive-bombing.

Neil received good marks in most of these disciplines, so he qualified for the next and hardest stage of training: carrier landings. Bringing a plane in to land on the short flight deck of an aircraft carrier is one of the biggest challenges for any naval pilot. Many pilots joke that "a good carrier landing is one from which you can walk away. A great carrier landing is one after which you can use the aircraft again."

For Neil, his first carrier landing was as emotional as his first solo back in Wapakoneta, and another major milestone in his life as an aviator.

It is certainly a very precise kind of flying. It works because you, in a very precise manner, get the airplane through that very small window that will allow it to land successfully on a very short flight deck.

His basic training over, Neil now moved on to advanced training. He was assigned to train on fighters, as he had requested, and the fighter plane he was allocated was the Grumman F8F-1 Bearcat. Neil was delighted with the plane, which was small, powerful, agile, and very fast. Following his first flight on March 28, 1950, Neil quickly mastered the Bearcat, guiding it in for six successful carrier landings.

Aircraft Fact File

Name:	Grumman F8F-1 Bearcat
Type:	Carrier-based fighter aircraft
Length:	28 ft. 3 in. (8.6 m)
Wingspan:	35 ft. 10 in. (10.9 m)
Top speed:	421 mph (678 kmh)
Rate of climb:	4,570 ft./min. (23.2 m/s)

On August 16, 1950, Neil received a letter confirming that he had successfully completed the course to become a naval aviator. Viola and June drove the 825 miles (1,328 km) to attend Neil's graduation ceremony on August 23. Neil went home with them for a short leave before reporting back for duty. He wondered where he would be posted. Two months earlier, on June 25, a war had broken out in Korea, and America had become involved. Neil suspected it wouldn't be long before he would be sent out there.

CHAPTER 3

THE HEAT OF BATTLE

Neil was assigned to Fighter Squadron 51, the first all-jet squadron in the US Navy. At just twenty years old, Neil was its youngest member. Yet the commanding officer, Lieutenant Commander Ernest Beauchamp, had watched Neil in training and was impressed. At the time of his appointment, Neil had yet to fly a jet, and he was thrilled to get the chance. Jets were a fairly new technology when Neil was assigned to one in 1951.

How Does a Jet Engine Work?

The turbojet engine (to give it its full name) works as follows: a fan at the front sucks in cold air; then a second fan called a compressor squeezes the air, increasing its temperature and pressure. Fuel squirted into the engine mixes with the compressed air and combusts. Hot waste gases from the combustion flow through a turbine, accelerating them. The gases then exit the engine at high speed through an exhaust nozzle, giving the engine its thrust.

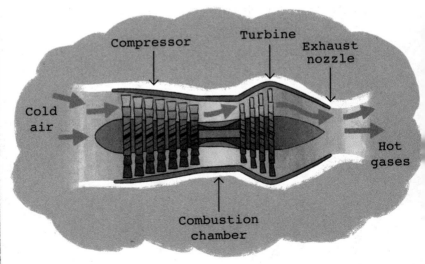

The first jet plane, the Heinkel He 178, had launched in 1939, just twelve years earlier. The thought of flying a jet made Neil feel a little like a pioneer—like one of his childhood heroes. He got his first chance to fly one on January 5, 1951, when he took up a Grumman F9F Panther. It was another "magic moment" in his flying life.

≥ FLYING A PANTHER ≤

The squadron was based on a 24,600-ton aircraft carrier, the USS *Essex*, moored off the coast of California. Carrier landings in the Panther were even more challenging than in the Bearcat, because the Panther was a lot faster. Neil would approach the flight deck as slowly as he could manage without stalling the engine, which was around 120 miles (193 km) per hour. Coming in at that speed, everything happened very fast. He had to drop steeply and make sure his tailhook snagged one of the "arresting wires" stretched across the deck, which jerked the Panther to a bone-shakingly sudden halt. If landings could be tense, takeoffs were nothing short of exhilarating: the aircraft was sent hurtling into the sky by a powerful hydraulic catapult. This method of takeoff was called a "cat shot."

When he wasn't training, Neil found his own ways to relax, building model airplanes and reading. This may have marked him out as unusual, but Neil gained the respect of his companions. One of them, Wam Mackey, described Neil as "a fine young pilot—a very solid aviator, very reliable."

Aircraft Fact File

Name:	Grumman F9F Panther
Type:	Carrier-based jet fighter
Length:	37 ft. 5 in. (11.4 m)
Wingspan:	38 ft. (11.6 m)
Top speed:	575 mph (925 kmh)
Rate of climb:	5,140 ft./min. (26.1 m/s)

As the squadron trained, its members felt the shadow of the Korean War looming over them. They practiced their dogfighting tactics, thinking they might have to face Russian MiG-15s. Neil thought about the flying aces of World War I that he'd read about as a boy. Would this be his chance to match their exploits? On June 25, 1951, their orders came through. It turned out they would not be engaging in dogfights—instead they would be carrying out bombing raids on enemy targets. For Neil, this came as something of a disappointment—even though he knew it would have been tough to go up against those MiGs, which were faster than the Panthers and could climb more quickly.

Three days later, the *Essex* departed for the US naval base at Pearl Harbor, Hawaii. After spending July there, they sailed for Korea, dropping anchor about 70 miles (113 km) off the northeast coast of the peninsula.

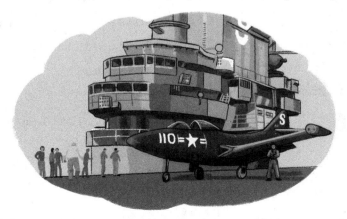

The Korean War

In 1945, the country of Korea was split into two nations. This was the era of the Cold War (see page 4). North Korea was supported by the Soviet Union and China, while South Korea was supported by the United States. The governments of both north and south insisted that they were the legitimate government of all Korea and viewed the other government as their enemy. On June 25, 1950, the conflict turned into open warfare when North Korean forces, supported by their allies, invaded the south. The United Nations voted to send a US-led force to help South Korea. After a war lasting more than three years, the North Korean forces were eventually driven back, and an armistice was signed.

Commander Beauchamp divided the squadron's twenty-four pilots into six divisions. Neil was placed in the sixth division, headed by John Carpenter. Neil flew mainly as Carpenter's wingman, meaning Neil's aircraft was positioned just behind and to the side of Carpenter's. Neil's first action in the war came on August 29, when he escorted a photoreconnaissance plane (a plane that observes and takes photographs of enemy positions) across the border into North Korea. This was followed by several combat missions. Squadron 51's objective was to damage the transport network that the North Korean and Chinese armies relied on.

Neil's ability to concentrate on the task and remain cool under pressure served him well during these missions. The only time he grew nervous was on some of the longer flights into enemy territory, when he feared he might run out of fuel before he could get back to the carrier.

⋛ BRUSH WITH DEATH ⋚

On September 3, Neil was on an armed reconnaissance mission into enemy territory when something happened that nearly cost him his life. The mission was to fly into a valley to the south of the village of Majon-ni, North Korea, and bomb gun sites, freight yards, trains, and a bridge. As the pilots flew in formation across the Sea of Japan, Neil could see his squadron mates in their planes alongside him, and he felt safer for their presence. He had great confidence in his Panther, too. When they got to the valley, they immediately ran into heavy anti-aircraft fire.

They never missed an opportunity to shoot at you. We saw all kinds of guns, all kinds of sizes, and some were radar-controlled. . . . There was always a lot of concern about getting hit. I had a lot of bullet holes in the airplanes I flew, but usually got [the airplanes] back.

As usual, Neil was flying as John Carpenter's wingman. Neil and his comrades dipped and dived to evade the guns. They opened fire, attacking the targets as bursts of flak (anti-aircraft fire) ripped the air around them. Neil knew that a direct hit from a shell could mean death. They managed to destroy all the targets except for the bridge, so Carpenter led his division into the valley once again. When Neil saw the bridge ahead, he fired his guns and released his bombs. Soon the bridge was nothing but rubble and twisted steel. As he began his climb, Neil saw too late a flash of cable. It was stretched hundreds of feet across the valley, placed there by the North Koreans to catch enemy aircraft. Neil's Panther was flying at 350 miles (563 km) per hour when it struck the cable, which sliced off almost 6 feet (1.8 m) of his right wing.

If you're going fast, a cable will make a very good knife!

The unbalanced plane started to roll. Neil had to think quickly. Having lost his right aileron, he had to raise the left aileron to full deflection just to keep the Panther stable. With his elevators damaged, he was rapidly losing height, so he used his trim tabs (thin, adjustable surfaces on the edges of his elevators). "Get up!" he cried as the plane continued to fall. Just before it hit the ground, the Panther's nose began, very slowly, to rise. Once he had climbed to a safer height, Neil radioed Carpenter and explained the problem. The Panther couldn't fly slower than 170 miles (274 km) per hour without rolling. It would mean a very fast landing on the *Essex*. Carpenter said the carrier couldn't handle anything at that speed. They agreed that Neil had to eject.

Escorted by Carpenter, Neil just about managed to fly the damaged plane back to friendly territory. He ejected close to Pohang Airfield on Korea's eastern coast, intending to splash down in the bay and await rescue by helicopters. However, the wind blew him inland, and he came down in a rice paddy. Apart from a sore tailbone from the ejection seat, he was unhurt. Within minutes, a jeep arrived. To Neil's amazement, the driver of the jeep was Goodell Warren, one of his roommates from flight school. Goodell, who was now a marine lieutenant at Pohang Airfield. He told Neil that

the bay was full of mines placed by the North Koreans, so it was lucky he hadn't come down there.

When Neil returned to the *Essex* the following evening, his comrades welcomed him back with some good-natured teasing, though several also expressed admiration at his cool handling of the situation. Celebrations were muted, however, because two more of their squadron had been killed in action that day. One of them, James Ashford, had been in Neil's division, and Neil may well have been on the same mission if he hadn't had his accident the day before.

DISASTER ON THE *ESSEX*

On September 16, 1951, John Keller, a junior officer in Squadron 172, suffered a midair collision in his F2H Banshee. Struggling to keep the jet fighter under control, he radioed to the *Essex* requesting an emergency landing. Unfortunately, Keller forgot to lower his tailhook as he came in. The Banshee struck the deck at nearly 150 miles (241 km) per hour. It careered through the crash barriers and smashed into a number of aircraft, some of which had pilots in them. Hundreds of gallons of fuel were ignited, causing a huge fireball. In total, seven men died, including Keller; sixteen were seriously injured; and eight jets were destroyed.

Neil was serving as squadron duty officer that day, so he was belowdecks in the ready room when it happened. He and his squadron mates mourned the loss of their comrades. As they gathered for a memorial service on September 20, Neil reflected on how lucky he had been. He had already survived losing part of his wing on his September 3 flight, and if he hadn't been serving as squadron duty officer thirteen days later, he would most likely have been on deck in one of the Panthers.

On September 21, the *Essex* docked at the Japanese port of Yokosuka for repairs, and the crew relaxed for ten days. Neil tried his hand at golf at the hotel where they were staying, and discovered he really enjoyed it. On October 1, they headed back to Korea.

In mid-October 1951, Neil was on early-morning combat patrol when he passed over a ridge of low mountains and saw below him hundreds of North Korean soldiers. They were unarmed, doing their morning workouts. Neil could have opened fire on them—he had his finger on the trigger—but instead he simply flew on. He didn't tell anyone about this until many years later. His squadron mates found out only after he died in 2012. One commented: "[There was] something too honorable in Neil for him to kill men who were in no position to defend themselves."

≡ DEATH OF A FRIEND ≡

Neil continued to fly and fight bravely for the rest of the war. His division attacked and destroyed numerous railways, supply depots, and bridges. Four more pilots from Squadron 51 died on combat missions in early 1952. The death that was the most difficult for Neil was that of Leonard "Chet" Cheshire. Neil and Chet had slept across the aisle from each other on the lower bunks, and they had become close friends. Chet, who was from Albuquerque, New Mexico, had gotten married just before his departure for Korea. He'd told Neil he planned to be a teacher when the war was over. On January 26, 1952, Chet's division was attacking a bridge near Wonsan in North Korea when his plane was hit by anti-aircraft fire and he was killed.

Attacking the Bridges

Bridges were especially well defended by the North Koreans, and many pilots were killed during these attacks. Over time, the navy discovered the most effective way of destroying bridges was a three-stage attack:

1. The jet fighters would drop in at a steep angle, firing at the bridge defenses and drawing anti-aircraft (AA) fire.
2. Next, the Corsair fighter planes would bomb and strafe the AA positions.
3. Finally, the Skyraider planes would bomb the bridge.

A total of twenty-four planes would be involved in a single bridge strike: eight jets, eight Corsairs, and eight Skyraiders.

≳ HOME AGAIN ≲

Neil's final flight of the war came on March 5, 1952. In total, he flew seventy-eight missions, amounting to 121 hours in the air. On March 11, the *Essex* set sail for Hawaii, and by March 25, it was back in California. Neil received numerous medals for his military service:

- → the Air Medal for his first twenty combat missions
- → two Gold Stars for the next forty combat missions
- → the Korean Service Medal and Engagement Star
- → the National Defense Service Medal
- → the United Nations Korea Medal

Neil was characteristically modest about all this, saying, "They handed out medals there like gold stars at Sunday school." Although the navy released him from active duty in August 1952, he remained in the reserves until 1960.

CHAPTER 4
TO THE LIMITS

Neil returned for his second spell at Purdue University in September 1952. He had only just turned twenty-two, but his experience in the Korean War had matured him. He took his studies more seriously and achieved even better grades than before.

Neil also became more involved in the social side of university life. He joined the Phi Delta Theta fraternity and lived in its fraternity house. He sang in Phi Delta's musical program and became its musical director. As part of a student revue, Neil wrote and co-directed two musicals, *Snow White and the Seven Dwarves* and *The Land of Egelloc* (*college* spelled backward). He also kept up his baritone horn, playing in the Purdue All-American Marching Band.

≥ FIRST LOVE ≤

Neil met his first serious girlfriend, Janet "Jan" Shearon, at a party while he was at Purdue. She was an eighteen-year-old home economics student. He met her again one early morning while she was on her way to the home economics laboratory and he was delivering the campus newspaper. He was attracted to her self-confidence, intelligence, and lively personality. Later that day, he told his roommate that he'd just met the girl he was going to marry. However, it wouldn't be until after he graduated in 1955 that he finally asked her out on a date. As Janet said later, "Neil isn't one to rush into anything."

Despite Neil's initial caution, the relationship quickly became serious. On January 28, 1956, they got married in a church in Janet's hometown of Wilmette, Illinois. Dean was Neil's best man, and June was one of Janet's attendants. In 1957, Neil and Janet bought a mountainside cabin in Juniper Hills, California, overlooking Antelope Valley.

EXPLORING THE FRONTIERS

Neil graduated from Purdue in January 1955 and was faced with the difficult choice of what to do next. He could:

- → continue in the navy
- → become a pilot for a civil airline
- → do graduate work in aeronautical engineering
- → become a research pilot

In the end, Neil decided to become a research pilot, testing high-speed, high-altitude experimental planes. This appealed to him because not only would he be flying planes, he would also be helping to advance the science and technology of flight. Like his heroes Alcock, Brown, Earhart, and Lindbergh, he would be exploring the frontiers of what was possible in aviation.

On July 11, 1955, Neil began work as a research pilot at Edwards Air Force Base in Southern California. Here, he found himself among the nation's elite pilots, many of them World War II veterans. However, it didn't take them long to see what a capable flyer Neil was and accept him as their equal.

One of his jobs was to copilot a B-29 Superfortress. The huge bomber would have a research aircraft attached to its undercarriage, which it would "air-launch." This was necessary because the research aircraft needed to be going at a certain speed before it could take off, or else its engine would stall. It couldn't reach that speed on the ground, so it had to be launched from another plane midair.

Aircraft Fact File

Name:	Boeing B-29 Superfortress
Type:	Four-engine, propeller-driven heavy bomber
Length:	99 ft. (30.2 m)
Wingspan:	141 ft. 3 in. (43.1 m)
Max take-off weight:	140,000 lb. (63,503 kg)
Top speed:	357 mph (575 kmh)

⇉ DANGER AT 30,000 FEET ⇇

Air-launches could be challenging and dangerous. The research aircraft added a lot of extra drag to the B-29, which had be taken up to 30,000 feet (9.1 km) or higher to be in the right position for the launch. This meant pushing the B-29 to the very limits of its capabilities. On March 22, 1956, Neil and copilot Stan Butchart were in a B-29. Their job was to launch a D-558-2 Skyrocket slung beneath them, piloted by Jack McKay. As they approached 30,000 feet (9.1 km), the B-29's number-four engine failed. This wasn't a major problem, as the B-29 could fly on three engines. The problem was that the plane was now doing less than 210 miles (338 km) per hour, which was too slow for the air launch. At this speed, the Skyrocket's engine would stall. The other problem was that the propeller on the broken engine was now windmilling wildly and could fly loose at any moment, potentially smashing into the Skyrocket.

Neil and Stan decided they had to launch the Skyrocket, which meant they needed to find some extra speed from somewhere. The only way they could do this was by putting the B-29 into a dive. Neil maneuvered the big plane into a steep angle of descent. When Stan judged they were going fast enough, he pulled the release lever. There was a huge roar as the Skyrocket launched. As it did so, the broken engine exploded.

Pieces of propeller flew in all directions. One sliced into the bomb bay where pilot Jack McKay had been sitting seconds earlier. Other pieces struck the number-two and number-three engines. The cables to the ailerons were snapped, so they lost some steering control. Flying with just one engine, Neil and Stan made a slow, circling descent before making an emergency landing in a lake bed.

≥ FAMILY TRAGEDY ≤

Neil and Jan's first child, Eric ("Ricky"), was born on June 30, 1957. Karen followed on April 13, 1959. But in 1961, two-year-old Karen began to get ill. She kept tripping, and her eyes would get crossed. She was taken to the hospital, where the doctors did several tests on her. Sadly, X-rays showed that Karen had a tumor in her brain.

She was given radiation treatment to reduce the size of the tumor, but this made her weak. Eventually she couldn't walk or even stand. Janet and Neil took turns staying with her at the hospital so she was never alone. "She was the sweetest thing," said Janet. "She never, ever complained."

Gradually, Karen improved and learned to walk again, and could even come home on weekends. But before long, the symptoms returned: crossed eyes and slurred speech. In her weakened state, Karen couldn't take any further treatment. Instead of keeping her in the hospital, everyone agreed she would be happier spending her final weeks at home. By now it was December, and the Armstrongs tried to make it an extra-special Christmas for her.

Karen enjoyed herself, but after Christmas, her condition worsened. She was back to crawling now, and soon she could no longer keep her food down. On January 28, 1962, Karen died at the family home in Juniper Hills.

Both Janet and Neil were devastated by the loss of their daughter. Neil dealt with his sorrow by throwing himself into his work. Everyone was surprised to see him back flying planes on February 6, but that was just his way of coping with it.

On April 8, 1963, Neil and Jan had their third and final child, a son named Mark.

THE PILOT-ENGINEER

During his seven years at Edwards Air Force Base, Neil made well over nine hundred flights and logged some 2,600 hours of flight time in many of the world's fastest, riskiest, and most experimental aircraft. For Neil, it was all for the purpose of engineering and solving the problems of flight. "We used airplanes like the mathematician might use a computer," he said, "as a tool to find answers in aerodynamics."

Typically, pilots at Edwards flew seat-of-the-pants-style, trusting their instincts to get themselves out of trouble. Neil was different. He understood how planes worked, and if something went wrong, he always wanted to know why. Most people he worked and flew with believed that his engineering background made him a better pilot.

THE EDGE OF SPACE

One of the most remarkable airplanes Neil flew during his time as a research pilot was the X-15. This rocket-powered aircraft was designed for super-fast speeds—more than six times the speed of sound. It could also fly extremely high, to the very edges of Earth's atmosphere, where it starts to fade into space. On April 20, 1962, Neil made his sixth flight in the X-15, and it would prove his most dramatic.

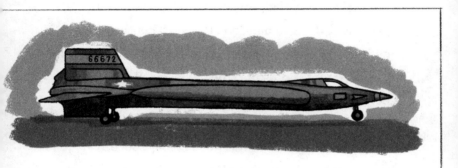

Aircraft Fact File

Name: North American X-15
Type: Hypersonic, rocket-powered experimental aircraft
Length: 50 ft. 9 in. (15.5 m)
Top speed: 4,520 mph (7,274 kmh)—world record for any piloted aircraft
Rate of climb: 60,000 ft./min. (304.8 m/s)
Highest flight: 67.0 mi. (108 km)

Neil was launched by a B-29 over Mud Lake, Nevada. He fired his rocket engine and shot upward. The X-15 accelerated to 3,789 miles (6,098 km) per hour, more than five times the speed of sound. When the fuel ran out after around eighty-two seconds, Neil shut off the engine, and the X-15 continued to ascend on its own momentum. It reached a peak of 207,500 feet (63.2 km)—the highest Neil ever flew before becoming an astronaut.

Up there, the views were spectacular—Neil could see the curvature of Earth. This was virtually space, and there was hardly any air, so Neil steered the X-15 using rocket thrusters, just like a spacecraft!

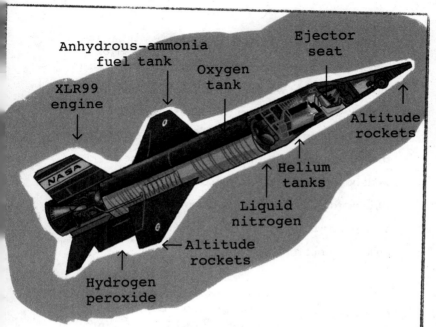

Flying Above the Air

Pilots flying within the atmosphere steer their aircraft using "aerodynamic control surfaces," such as the rudder, elevators, and ailerons. The pilot manipulates these surfaces, and the airflow around them changes, causing the plane to go up, go down, or turn. But at the edge of space there isn't enough air for these control surfaces to work, so the X-15 is maneuvered by means of rocket thrusters.

After reaching the top of its arc of flight, the X-15 began to descend toward the atmosphere. Part of Neil's job with this flight was to test out the X-15's new control system, so at 100,000 feet (30.5 km) he lifted the nose slightly, angling the craft upward. But when he did this, the X-15 bounced off the top of the atmosphere and went ballooning back up to 115,000 feet (35.1 km). At Edwards Air Force Base, they saw on the radar that something was wrong and radioed Neil: "We see you ballooning, not turning. Hard left turn, Neil!"

I tried to turn, but nothing was working because there was no air around me.

With no air, the control surfaces didn't work, so the X-15 continued hurtling forward on its own momentum. Using the rocket thrusters, Neil eventually managed to roll the craft over and drop back into the atmosphere. He turned toward Edwards, but unfortunately he was now 45 miles (72.4 km) farther south than he should have been. There was a real danger he wouldn't be able to reach the dry lake at Edwards Base, where he could land.

Landing an X-15

Because the X-15 used up all its fuel during the ascent, the pilot had to land it unpowered. This meant the craft became, in effect, a glider. But unlike ordinary gliders, the X-15's wingspan was shorter than its body length, so it didn't glide very well! The pilot had to bring it down in a wide, circling descent, slowing its speed to just 230 mph (370 kmh) at landing. And with no power, the pilot had just one chance to get it right!

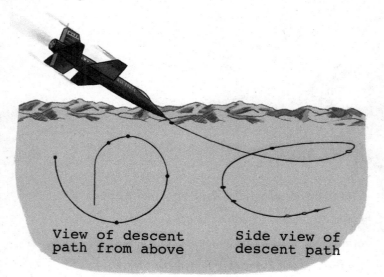

View of descent path from above

Side view of descent path

Neil knew there weren't any safe lake beds in the area for an emergency landing. There was a small airport nearby, but he couldn't be sure if there was a clear runway, and he would have only one chance to land. Also, the X-15 had metal skids instead of wheels. These were great for landing on the dry mud of a lake bed, but a concrete runway might rip them to shreds. Neil had no choice but to try to get back to Edwards.

He reached the southern edge of the lake bed with little to spare. Witnesses who watched the landing claimed he came swooping in level with the Joshua trees that grew at the edge of the lake bed.

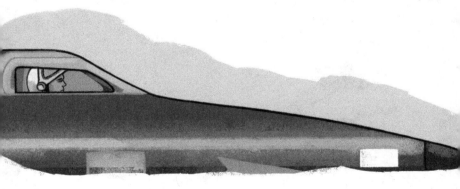

Neil's adventure in the X-15 became the stuff of legend at Edwards. People jokingly called it his "cross-country flight." At 12 minutes and 28.7 seconds, it was also the longest flight ever made in an X-15.

CHAPTER 5

JOURNEY INTO SPACE

While Neil Armstrong was working as a research pilot, testing the limits of aircraft at the very edges of the atmosphere, another program was being developed to take humans even deeper into space. In October 1958, NASA announced the launch of Project Mercury. Its goal was to put a man into Earth orbit and return him safely.

Mercury astronauts had to be military pilots, so Neil as a civilian was ineligible (being in the reserves was not enough). But in April 1962, NASA announced that it wished to recruit a second group of astronauts for a new spaceflight program called Project Gemini, and this time civilians could apply.

NASA NEEDS YOU!
APPLY NOW FOR
PROJECT GEMINI
Civilian Applications Welcomed

Project Gemini

The purpose of Project Gemini was to develop space-travel techniques that would be needed for the Apollo program, which aimed to land astronauts on the moon. Two of the critical techniques that needed to be developed were:

- extra-vehicular activity (EVA)—when astronauts leave the spacecraft in their spacesuits to work outside it

- space rendezvous and docking—when two spacecraft join together in orbit

⇉ BECOMING AN ASTRONAUT ⇇

Two months earlier, Mercury astronaut John Glenn had become the first American to orbit Earth. His achievement had captured the public imagination like nothing since Charles Lindbergh's famous transatlantic flight in 1927. Neil saw there was real excitement surrounding NASA's space program, and he wondered if he should be part of it. However, he delayed sending in his application and missed the June 1 deadline by about a week.

Luckily, a man named Dick Day was one of the people in charge of selecting the new astronauts. He had worked with Neil at Edwards, and he thought him better qualified than anyone to be an astronaut. When Neil's application came in, Day slipped it into the pile with all the other applications so no one would realize it was late. In September 1962, Neil was thrilled to learn that he had been selected as one of the new astronauts.

I've Got a Secret

A few days after Neil heard he was going to be an astronaut, NASA told his parents the news. NASA then arranged for Stephen and Viola to be invited onto a popular television show called *I've Got a Secret*. One of the panelists on the show managed to guess the Armstrongs' secret—their son had just become an astronaut. The show's host then showed remarkable foresight when he asked Viola, "Now, how would you feel, Mrs. Armstrong, if it turned out . . . that your son is the first man to land on the moon?" Viola replied, "Well, I guess I'd just say, God bless him and I wish him the best of all good luck."

⋛ THE NEW NINE ⋚

The "New Nine," as the second group of astronauts was known, were put through a tough training schedule:

- They were exposed to acceleration, vibration, and noise to simulate the experience of being in a space capsule.
- They went on jungle and desert survival camps.
- They kept up their cockpit skills by making regular flights in rocket-powered aircraft.
- They made parachute jumps on land and into water.
- They spent time in microgravity, learning how to move, use tools, eat, and drink in near-weightless conditions.

⋛ A SPIN THROUGH SPACE ⋚

In September 1965, three years after becoming an astronaut, Neil was finally given his first mission in space. He was assigned command of NASA's fourteenth crewed space mission, Gemini 8. His crewmate would be a thirty-three-year-old Texan named Dave Scott.

For Neil and Dave, the mission was well worth waiting for, because Gemini 8 was to perform the first docking between two spacecraft in history. Also, the plan was that Dave would perform a two-hour, ten-minute EVA. This was much longer than Ed White's twenty-minute spacewalk in June of that year on Gemini 4. From the time of their assignment until launch day six months later, Neil and Dave trained exclusively for the mission.

On March 16, 1966, the two men entered the *Gemini 8* space capsule at Cape Kennedy in Florida. Janet stayed at home with the two boys, watching the events unfold on television. Neil's parents, as well as Dean and June, were in the VIP viewing stands in Florida. They all watched nervously as the Titan II rocket lifted smoothly into the sky, carrying Neil and Dave into space.

The rocket's acceleration exerted powerful g-forces on the astronauts, perhaps up to 7 g (seven times Earth's normal gravity), but they both had practiced for this in a machine known as a centrifuge, and they knew their bodies could handle it. Soon, the blue sky had darkened to black. The thunderous vibrations of the rocket engine ceased, and they were floating silently in orbit. Looking out of the window, they saw spectacular views of the Pacific Ocean and the islands of Hawaii.

Their plan was to dock with an uncrewed spacecraft called the Agena, which had launched a little earlier. They consulted the onboard computer, which was tracking the Agena via radar. Neil fired *Gemini 8*'s thrusters to send it into the same orbit as the Agena's.

While they waited for the Agena to appear, Neil and Dave ate a meal of freeze-dried chicken-and-gravy casserole. Then Neil opened a package of brownies, but in the weightless conditions, the crumbs floated all around the cabin.

After their meal, there was nothing to do but wait. For a long time, they couldn't see the Agena. . . .

Six and a half hours after launch, Neil radioed Mission Control in Houston: "Flight, we are docked! Yes, it's really a smoothie." Huge celebrations broke out at Mission Control over the world's first space docking.

Shortly afterward, Mission Control lost contact with the astronauts as *Gemini 8*-Agena moved out of range of the tracking station. By the time contact resumed twenty-one minutes later, something had gone terribly wrong. Dave Scott's anxious voice came on the radio: "We have serious problems here. We're . . . we're tumbling end over end up here."

What had happened was this: Shortly after losing contact with Mission Control, *Gemini 8*-Agena went into a thirty-degree tilt. Nothing Dave or Neil tried could solve this. Both astronauts agreed that the fault probably lay with the Agena. But when they undocked, it only made matters worse. *Gemini 8* started to spin out of control. Unknown to them, one of the spacecraft's thrusters had become stuck in the "on" position.

With each rotation they went faster and faster. Soon they were spinning once every second. The astronauts were getting dizzy. Neil tried to keep the control panel in focus, but his vision was becoming blurry. He knew they would have to do something quickly before they lost consciousness. When Dave finally managed to get through to Mission Control, they were mystified.

In the end, it was Neil's coolness under pressure that saved them. He decided to switch off all the thrusters and activate the spacecraft's other control system, the one used for re-entry. This way, they were able to regain control of *Gemini 8* and stop the spin.

Mission rules dictated that once the re-entry control system had been activated, the crew had to be brought home. So the mission was cut short and, unfortunately, Dave Scott never got to perform his EVA. After making one final orbit, they re-entered the atmosphere, splashing down in the Pacific Ocean ten hours and forty-one minutes after liftoff.

After an investigation, it was agreed that the crew could not be blamed for the accident and in fact had shown remarkable piloting skills in the circumstances. Both men received NASA's Distinguished Service Medal.

The Apollo Program

The rest of the Gemini flights went well. So in early 1967, NASA launched the Apollo program, which would take astronauts to the moon. NASA scientists had come up with various options for achieving this. The one they decided upon involved several stages:

1. A three-stage Saturn V rocket fires the astronauts into Earth orbit, burning up its first two stages in the process.
2. A command/service module, together with a lunar module, detaches from the Saturn V's third stage and flies to the moon.
3. Once in lunar orbit, the lunar module detaches from the command/service module and lands astronauts on the moon.
4. After the lunar module leaves the lunar surface and docks with the command/service module, the astronauts return to Earth.

⪦ FLYING WITHOUT WINGS ⪧

The most complex piece of technology in all this was the lunar module. No one had ever designed a machine to land on the moon, which has one-sixth of Earth's gravity. The astronauts wanted to rehearse this part of the mission, but it was difficult to reproduce the conditions on Earth. Eventually, NASA came up with a machine for this purpose called a Lunar Landing Training Vehicle (LLTV). The LLTV was a wingless aircraft, powered by a turbofan engine, that took off and landed vertically.

Once it had reached the desired altitude, the pilot would lower the throttle to support just five-sixths of the vehicle's weight (to simulate the moon's one-sixth gravity), then try to land it using a system of small rockets and thrusters.

The LLTV, an ungainly machine nicknamed the "flying bedstead," was unstable and dangerous. Yet Neil knew it was the only mechanism they could use to rehearse for a moon landing, and he ended up making more flights in it than any other astronaut.

> "Without wings, [the LLTV] could not glide to a safe landing if the main engine or the thrusters failed. And to train on it properly, an astronaut had to fly at altitudes of up to five hundred feet. At that height, a glitch could be fatal."
> —Buzz Aldrin

On May 6, 1968, Neil was in an LLTV about 100 feet (30 m) above the ground when he began to lose control. The vehicle tilted at wild angles as it started to plummet. Neil quickly realized that he wasn't going to be able to stop it from crashing, so he ejected. He drifted down in his parachute as the LLTV exploded in flames beneath him. Later analysis showed that if he'd ejected half a second later, his parachute wouldn't have opened in time. His only injury came from having bitten his tongue during ejection.

Neil's reaction to the accident was typical: he went back to his office and got on with his work. Another astronaut, Alan Bean, having heard what happened, raced in to ask him about it. Bean relates the story: "I said, 'I heard that you bailed out of the LLTV an hour ago.' [Neil] thought for a second and said, 'Yeah, I did.'" Bean was amazed: "Offhand, I can't think of another person, let alone another astronaut, who would have just gone back to his office after ejecting a fraction of a second before getting killed."

APOLLO COMMAND

Following the tragedy of *Apollo 1* (see page 10), the Apollo program proceeded smoothly. In December 1968, the world watched, awestruck, as Apollo 8 astronauts Frank Borman, Jim Lovell, and Bill Anders became the first humans to break free of Earth's gravity and go into orbit around the moon.

And then, on January 4, 1969, Neil received some incredible news. He had been assigned command of Apollo 11, the mission that would attempt to actually land humans on the moon.

CHAPTER 6
ONE GIANT LEAP

Neil's crewmates for Apollo 11 would be Edwin "Buzz" Aldrin and Mike Collins. Like Neil, they were both born in 1930 and were experienced pilots and astronauts. Buzz was a trained engineer and veteran fighter pilot from the Korean War. As a crew member of Gemini 12, Buzz had performed a five-hour EVA. For Apollo 11, he would be lunar module pilot. Mike, a former test pilot, had been on the Gemini 10 mission, during which he performed two rendezvous with different spacecraft and two EVAs. Mike would be command module pilot on Apollo 11. He would remain aboard the command/service module, orbiting the moon, while Neil and Buzz headed down to the surface in the lunar module.

⋛ PREPARATION AND LAUNCH ⋚

During the six months leading up to the launch, all three men trained hard for the mission. They spent much of this time in flight simulators of the command and lunar modules, rehearsing the critical tasks they would need to perform up in space. On one occasion, Neil crashed the lunar module simulator rather than abort the landing, making Buzz very angry, but generally they got along well.

At a press conference on July 5, 1969, eleven days before the launch, Neil announced the names they had decided upon for the parts of the spacecraft. The command module would be *Columbia*, and the lunar module would be *Eagle*.

The day of the launch finally arrived on July 16, 1969. The astronauts were woken at 4:15 a.m. After breakfast, they climbed into their space suits and were driven the short distance to the launchpad at Cape Kennedy. Though they were excited, the astronauts understood the mission was a risky one. Neil estimated their chances of getting back alive at no higher than fifty-fifty.

Dangers of Space Travel

In space: there is no air, food, or water. It is a place of freezing and boiling temperatures. If astronauts are to survive, they must be protected from extremes of temperature, pressure, radiation, and micrometeorites.

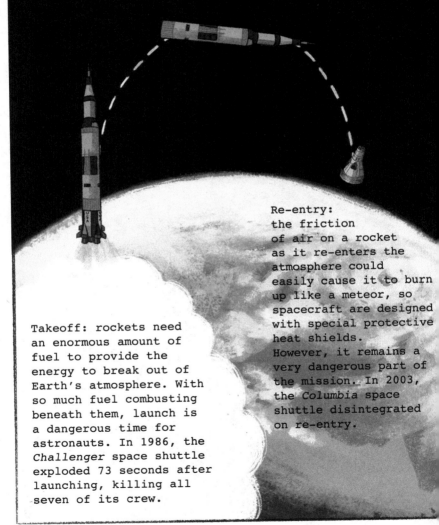

Re-entry: the friction of air on a rocket as it re-enters the atmosphere could easily cause it to burn up like a meteor, so spacecraft are designed with special protective heat shields. However, it remains a very dangerous part of the mission. In 2003, the *Columbia* space shuttle disintegrated on re-entry.

Takeoff: rockets need an enormous amount of fuel to provide the energy to break out of Earth's atmosphere. With so much fuel combusting beneath them, launch is a dangerous time for astronauts. In 1986, the *Challenger* space shuttle exploded 73 seconds after launching, killing all seven of its crew.

It was a bright Florida morning. Around a million spectators had gathered on nearby beaches and highways to watch the launch. There were also seven thousand official spectators seated in grandstands, and a worldwide audience of millions watching live on television.

Memento

Neil took a special memento with him on board Apollo 11: a chip of wood from the propeller and a piece of fabric from the wing of the Wright Flyer, the first successful airplane, built by his earliest heroes, the Wright brothers.

Exactly on schedule, the giant Saturn V rocket thundered into the sky on a plume of smoke and flame. Inside the command module, the noise and vibration of the first stage rocket was overwhelming. The second and third stages were far smoother and quieter. Mike said the Saturn V turned into a "gentle giant." Twelve minutes after launch, they went into orbit. After circling Earth one and a half times, they fired up the third-stage engine once again, accelerating *Apollo 11* to over 24,000 miles (38,624 km) per hour in order to escape Earth's gravity.

Timeline of Launch

(Times are Eastern Daylight Time.)

09:32 a.m	*Apollo 11* launches.
09:34 a.m.	At a height of 44 mi. (70.8 km), Stage 1 of the Saturn V rocket falls away.
09:41 a.m.	Stage 2 falls away. *Apollo 11* is now traveling at 22,370 mph (36,001 kmh).
09:44 a.m.	*Apollo 11*, now 103 mi. (166 km) high, enters Earth orbit.
12:22 p.m.	Stage 3 rockets reignite to put *Apollo 11* on course for the moon.

JOURNEY TO THE MOON

Twenty-five minutes later, Mike separated *Columbia* from Saturn's third stage and turned it around. At the top of the third stage, inside a protective container, was *Eagle*. The container opened, and Mike carefully docked head-to-head with *Eagle*. Once the docking was complete, the third stage was jettisoned, and the combined *Columbia-Eagle* continued on its journey to the moon. The spacecraft rotated slowly as it flew so that the sun's rays didn't heat one side for too long. This rotation gave the crew ever-changing, beautiful views of the receding Earth and the approaching moon.

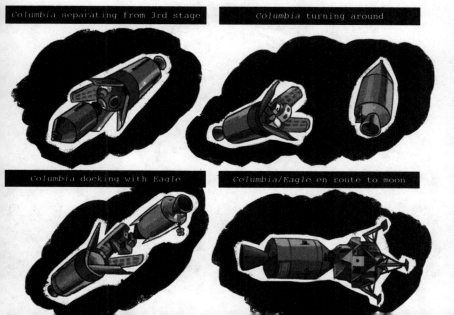

Columbia separating from 3rd stage

Columbia turning around

Columbia docking with Eagle

Columbia/Eagle en route to moon

> "We were like a chicken on a barbecue spit. If we stopped in one position for too long, all sorts of bad things could happen."
> —Mike Collins

Soon it was time to eat their first meal. The astronauts squirted water from a hot-water gun into bags of dry food to make it edible. Then they sucked up the food through a tube. Meals included turkey with gravy, and ham and potatoes. Neil's favorite was spaghetti with meat sauce, scalloped potatoes, pineapple fruitcake cubes, and grape punch.

Eleven hours into the flight, it was time for their first sleep period. Neil and Buzz slept in hammocks. Mike, the man on watch, drifted above them. A belt kept him from floating off, and he had a radio receiver taped to his ear in case Houston needed to call during the night. Mike enjoyed the floating sensation, describing it as being "suspended by a cobweb's light touch—just floating and falling all the way to the moon."

At 7:30 p.m. on day two, the crew gave a TV broadcast to the people watching back at home. Neil pointed the camera out the window to show them what Earth looks like from a distance of 139,244 miles (224,091 km). During the rest of the half-hour transmission, the crew tried its best to be entertaining. Buzz showed viewers how to do push-ups in weightless conditions, Neil stood on his head, and Mike demonstrated how to make chicken stew.

When the crew awoke on the morning of day four, the moon was a huge sphere filling the windows. It was now just over 12,000 miles (19,312 km) away. At 1:28 p.m., Mike fired the main engine for six minutes, slowing down *Apollo 11* so that it could be trapped in lunar orbit. Later that afternoon, the crew transmitted close-up TV images of the lunar surface.

The following day, July 20, 1969, Neil and Buzz crawled through the hatch into *Eagle* and started to power it up. It was time for them to land on the moon.

At 3:46 p.m., Mike radioed to them, "You cats take it easy down there on the lunar surface." Then he threw the switch to separate *Eagle* from *Columbia*.

While the two aircraft were still close to each other, Neil slowly rotated *Eagle* so Mike could inspect it.

Someone's upside down!

≡ LANDING ON THE MOON ≡

Neil Armstrong's entire life as a pilot had prepared him for what was to follow: the landing of *Eagle* on the moon. So many challenging experiences had helped make him the great pilot he was:

- → his first solo at Wapakoneta in the Aeronca Champion

- → losing half a wing in his Phantom fighter jet in Korea

- → his "cross-country" flight in the X-15

- → his wild spin in *Gemini 8*

- → his near miss in the "flying bedstead"

All these adventures and others had honed Neil's skills and instincts, making him the ideal person for the task he now faced. As it turned out, the landing would test even his nerve and ability. What was more, he would have to do it with the whole world watching.

Lunar Module

The lunar module *Eagle* consisted of an ascent stage (upper section) and a descent stage (lower section). The ascent stage contained the crew cabin and its own engine and fuel. When the crew was ready to leave, the ascent and descent stages would separate. The ascent-stage rocket would fire the astronauts back into orbit using the descent stage as a launch platform.

Neil and Buzz stood side by side at their control panels, watching through triangular windows as *Eagle* made its 60-mile (96.6-km) descent toward the lunar surface. At 4:08 p.m., Neil fired *Eagle*'s descent engine. He began tracking the surface landmarks to confirm *Eagle*'s flight path. They were heading for a landing zone in a part of the moon called the Sea of Tranquility. About three minutes into the powered descent, Neil noticed they were passing the landmarks two or three seconds early. "I think we're going a little long," he said.

Neither of them knew why this could be. Perhaps they'd started the descent engine a little late. Each second represented roughly one mile (1.6 km) of distance, so they were heading for quite a different landing spot than the one planned.

It wasn't a big deal as to exactly where we were going to set down. There wasn't going to be any welcoming committee there anyway.

Sea of Tranquility

When you look up at the moon at night, you will see several dark patches on its surface. Early astronomers mistook these for seas and gave them names such as the Sea of Tranquility. In fact, they are plains of basalt, a rock formed out of cooled, iron-rich lava from ancient volcanic eruptions. Basalt reflects less light than other kinds of rock, which is why these patches appear dark to us.

Neil turned *Eagle* into a more upright orientation to get the landing radar in position, so they could determine their altitude. At that moment, a computer alarm sounded. The screen flashed "1202." Neither Neil nor Buzz knew what 1202 meant. Nor did Charlie Duke at Mission Control. This hadn't come up in the simulations. Then Duke's colleague Steve Bales said, "It's okay, the computer's just saying it's got more than it can handle. It's not critical." It turned out, the computer had become temporarily overloaded with all the radar data coming in. The 1202 alarm soon changed to 1201. Again, Bales told them to ignore it. They did, but for Neil, all these alarms were a serious distraction when he needed to concentrate on the landing.

When Neil turned back to the window, what he saw worried him a great deal. They were now below 2,000 feet (610 m), and were heading toward the near slope of a crater. The crater was surrounded by a field of boulders, some of them the size of cars. Neil didn't want to land on the steep slope, and he needed to avoid those big rocks, too.

When they were at 500 feet (152 m), he took over manual control of *Eagle*. He slowed the descent by pitching the lunar module upright, but maintained its forward speed so he could fly beyond the crater. While Buzz read out the numbers for speed and height, Neil searched for a clear place to land. As they dropped below 100 feet (30 m), the descent engine began kicking up a lot of dust, obscuring the view.

Meanwhile, another problem had arisen: *Eagle* was running low on fuel in its descent engine. With little more than a minute's worth of fuel left in the tank, the astronauts would soon be forced to abort the landing, fire up the ascent engine, and return to *Columbia*. Charlie Duke warned them they had just thirty seconds of fuel remaining. Neil's instinct told him to ignore the warnings. This close to the ground, he figured he could land the *Eagle* unpowered if necessary. But first he had to find a place to land amid all these boulders. Finally, through the blanket of dust, he spotted a clear space ahead.

"Contact light," said Buzz, the signal for Neil to shut down the engine. Then, at 4:17 and 43 seconds, with just twenty seconds of fuel remaining, they landed. It was so soft, they barely realized they were down. But the view from the window confirmed it: Neil Armstrong and Buzz Aldrin had just become the first humans on the moon!

As soon as it was clear that they had landed safely, celebrations broke out around the world. "Whew, boy! Man on the moon!" exclaimed TV commentator Walter Cronkite. At the Armstrong home in Houston, Janet was watching it all with Ricky and Mark. Astronaut Bill Anders was there with them. They had their moon maps laid out and were following every second of the descent. Janet hugged her boys and let out a big sigh of relief at the moment of landing.

> "I was afraid the floor of the moon was going to be so unsafe for them. I was worried that they might sink in too deep. But no, they didn't. So it was wonderful."
> —Viola Armstrong

Preparations for the EVA took several hours. Finally, at 10:39 p.m., *Eagle*'s hatch opened. Ten minutes after that, Neil wriggled out and began descending the ladder toward the surface....

CHAPTER 7
RELUCTANT HERO

So here we are back at that moment with Neil taking his first step on the moon. At 10:56 and 15 seconds on July 20, 1969, he stepped off the ladder and became the first human to touch the surface of another world. The words he spoke then, which Neil said he thought up only after landing *Eagle*, captured this historic moment and became instantly famous. He said, "That's one small step for man, one giant leap for mankind." In fact, he didn't quite say it correctly. He'd planned to say "one small step for a man"—but everyone knew what he meant!

⋛ WALKING ON THE MOON ⋛

Buzz soon followed Neil out, and the two of them explored the lunar surface. "It has a stark beauty all its own," remarked Neil. Buzz described it as "magnificent desolation." The powdery soil was quite slippery, they discovered, but walking was no problem. They unveiled a commemorative plaque that had been mounted on *Eagle*'s base.

They planted a US flag, stiffened with wire to make it look like it was flying in a breeze. Neil photographed Buzz saluting it.

President Richard Nixon called them by radio-telephone from the White House. "This certainly has to be the most historic telephone call ever made," he said. "I just can't tell you how proud we all are of what you've done.... For one priceless moment in the whole history of man, all the people of this Earth are truly one."

Neil and Buzz spent the rest of the EVA collecting rock and soil samples and performing experiments. They set up devices to sense moonquakes and to measure the distance between the moon and Earth. Those devices would stay on the moon.

They spent about two and a half hours on the surface. Neil would have liked to stay longer and explore farther afield, but it was about 200 degrees Fahrenheit (93°C) on the surface, and no one knew how long the water that cooled their space suits would last. That was why NASA strictly limited their moonwalking time.

BUZZ AND THE FELT-TIP PEN

When they climbed back inside *Eagle*, Buzz noticed a switch lying on the floor. It must have broken off earlier when they were moving around in the cramped cabin. Unfortunately, it was the switch that fired the ascent engine. If they couldn't fix it, they would be stuck on the moon!

Buzz hunted around for something to use in place of the switch. Then he noticed a felt-tip pen, which he kept in his shoulder pocket. He tried inserting it in the opening where the switch should have been. To his and Neil's great relief, it fit. They would be able to leave the moon after all!

Neil and Buzz did more chores and got some well-earned rest. Then they prepared for departure. At 1:54 p.m. on July 21, they fired *Eagle*'s ascent engine and rose from the surface. *Eagle* docked with *Columbia* at 5:35 p.m., and a hugely relieved Mike welcomed them back aboard.

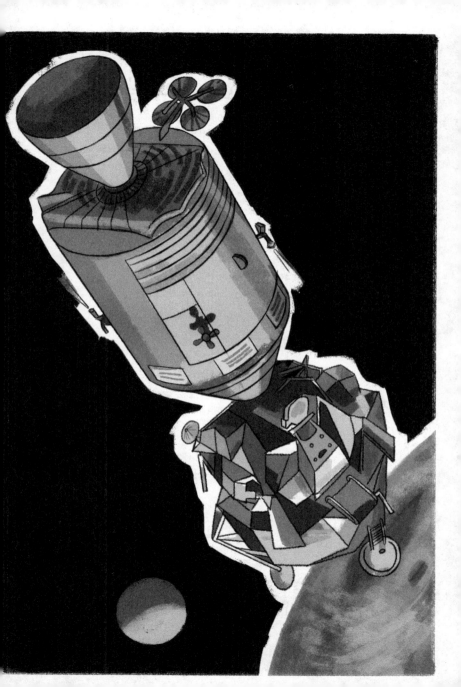

Some Corner of Another World

Plans had been made in the event of Neil and Buzz becoming stranded on the moon. President Nixon was going to read out a statement on television:

> Fate has ordained that the men who went to the moon to explore in peace will stay on the moon to rest in peace. These brave men, Neil Armstrong and Edwin Aldrin, know that there is no hope for their recovery. But they also know that there is hope for mankind in their sacrifice....

It would have ended with a line adapted from the poem "The Soldier" by Rupert Brooke:

> For every human being who looks up at the moon in the nights to come will know that there is some corner of another world that is forever mankind.

Mission Control would then have closed down communications with the lunar module and a clergyman would "commend their souls to the deepest of the deep," similar to a burial at sea.

Return Journey Timeline

July 21	7:42 p.m.	*Columbia* jettisons *Eagle*.
July 22	12:56 a.m.	*Columbia* leaves lunar orbit.
	9:08 p.m.	Live TV transmission begins.
July 23	3:56 p.m.	Midway point of journey home.
	7:03 p.m.	Final TV transmission begins.
July 24	12:21 p.m.	*Columbia* jettisons service module.
	12:35 p.m.	*Columbia* re-enters Earth's atmosphere.
	12:51 p.m.	*Columbia* splashes down in the Pacific Ocean.

SPLASHDOWN AND QUARANTINE

After an uneventful ride back to Earth, the astronauts splashed down southwest of Hawaii. They were picked up by helicopter and taken to the recovery ship, USS *Hornet*, where President Nixon was waiting to greet them. A brass band played, and sailors cheered as the astronauts were escorted into their quarantine trailer. This was a precaution in case they had picked up any unknown germs while on the moon. They would remain in quarantine for three weeks, most of it spent at the Lunar Receiving Laboratory in Houston.

Did They See a UFO?

While in quarantine, the Apollo 11 crew reported that shortly after nine p.m. on the third day of their journey, they saw something strange out of the window. It looked like a flying cylinder, around 100 miles (161 km) away. The official explanation was that they had seen one of the four panels that had enclosed *Eagle*, which had flown off in different directions when the lunar module was released. But could it have been a UFO? We'll never know.

⇃ CELEBRATIONS ⇂

Neil, Buzz, and Mike emerged from quarantine to discover they had become national heroes. The celebrations began on August 13 with ticker-tape parades through New York City and Chicago. Thousands of spectators lined the routes, cheering and applauding as the astronauts went by in open-top cars.

This was followed by a party in Los Angeles hosted by President Nixon, with many famous Hollywood stars in attendance. Neil, normally so calm, was overcome by emotion as he addressed the president. He said:

We were very privileged to leave on the moon a plaque endorsed by you, Mr. President, saying, "For all mankind". Perhaps in the third millennium a wayward stranger will read the plaque at Tranquility Base. We'll let history mark that this was the age in which that became a fact. I was struck this morning in New York by a proudly waved but uncarefully scribbled sign. It said: "Through you, we touched the moon." It was our privilege today to touch America.

On September 6, Wapakoneta put on a spectacular celebration for Neil and his family. The whole town came out to cheer their favorite son, and the Purdue University Marching Band provided music. Streets along the parade route were temporarily renamed in honor of Apollo 11.

End of the Space Race

By landing humans on the moon, the United States had effectively won the Space Race with the Soviet Union. Between 1969 and 1972, the Soviets made four attempts to land a craft on the moon, all of which failed. With the end of the Space Race, public interest in the lunar missions declined. Five more Apollo missions landed astronauts on the moon, the final one occurring in December 1972, but none received as much attention as Apollo 11. In 1975, an Apollo spacecraft docked in orbit with a Soviet Soyuz spacecraft. The commanders of the two spacecraft greeted each other with a famous "handshake in space," symbolizing a new era of cooperation between the two superpowers.

A few weeks after the lunar landing, the Apollo 11 astronauts and their wives set off on the so-called "Giant Leap" tour that would take them around the world. Over the next thirty-seven days, they visited twenty-seven cities on five continents. During the tour, they were seen by close to 150 million people and shook an estimated 25,000 hands. Although not comfortable with public speaking, Neil became the astronauts' official spokesperson, and always managed to find the right words for the occasion.

One of his favorite moments came in Paris on October 6, when a representative of the Aero Club of France presented its gold medal to the astronauts.

> I was honored to receive a medal previously only given to the Wright brothers and Charles Lindbergh from America.

Janet thought the trip was wonderful. She particularly remembered that during their visits to Amsterdam and Brussels, they met two kings and queens in one day!

WHAT NEXT?

Eventually, the celebrations and goodwill tours drew to a close, and the time came for Neil to decide what to do next. For a brief period, he worked for NASA's aeronautics team, where he helped develop the new technology of "fly by wire"—flying a plane semiautomatically with help from a computer. Then, in 1971, he left NASA and became a professor of aerospace engineering at the University of Cincinnati.

Neil turned out to be a very good teacher. He was popular with his students, even though he could be a tough grader. Toward the end of a semester, he would sometimes break off a lecture to entertain them with one of his flying stories.

Neil left teaching in 1979 in order to focus on his business activities. He served on the board of directors for several companies, and was a spokesman for the American car manufacturer Chrysler. He also found time for the occasional adventure. In April 1985, Neil made a trip to the North Pole. The expedition included several other famous explorers, including Edmund Hillary, the first to climb Everest; Steve Fossett, the first person to fly solo around the world in a balloon; and Patrick Morrow, the first person to climb the highest mountain on each of the world's continents.

In 1986, President Ronald Reagan invited Neil to join a commission to investigate the *Challenger* disaster. *Challenger* was a space shuttle that broke apart shortly after liftoff, killing all seven of the crew. The commission discovered it was due to the failure of a poorly designed pressure seal in one of the rocket motors.

⋛ DEALING WITH FAME ⋚

Neil was a modest man who did not enjoy the fame and adulation that came with being the first person on the moon. In a 2005 interview, he said, "I just don't deserve it. I wasn't chosen to be first. I was just chosen to command that flight. Circumstance put me in that particular role." The public didn't seem to agree. During the months that followed the moon landing, Neil was getting around ten thousand fan letters a day.

He tried to keep a low profile, not giving many interviews and declining requests for public appearances. In 1993, he discovered that people were selling his autograph for money, so he stopped signing things. As a result, Neil gained the reputation of being a recluse. But his friend and fellow astronaut John Glenn said, "[Neil] didn't feel that he should be out huckstering [selling] himself. He was a humble person, and that's the way he remained after his lunar flight."

≍ THE END ≍

Neil continued to enjoy an active life into his old age. He went skiing and played golf, and indulged his love of flying by piloting sailplanes, a type of glider. He traveled the world, giving speeches and attending events. He also spent lots of time with his family and with friends such as Kotcho Solacoff, whom he had remained close to since his days in Upper Sandusky. In 1994, Neil and Janet got divorced after thirty-eight years of marriage. The same year he married a widow from Cincinnati called Carol Held Knight.

On August 25, 2012, at the age of eighty-two, Neil died following heart surgery. Shortly afterward, his family issued a statement. This is part of it:

Neil was our loving husband, father, grandfather, brother, and friend. Neil Armstrong was also a reluctant American hero who always believed he was just doing his job. He served his nation proudly, as a navy fighter pilot, test pilot, and astronaut.

There were many other tributes to Neil:

"Neil was among the greatest of American heroes, not just of his time, but of all time."
—President Barack Obama

"He was a man who had all the courage in the world."
—Patrick Moore, astronomer

"As long as there are history books, Neil Armstrong will be included in them."
—Charles Bolden Jr., NASA administrator

"A true American hero and the best pilot I ever knew."
—Buzz Aldrin

"He was the best, and I will miss him terribly."
—Mike Collins

President Obama ordered all American flags to be lowered to half-mast until sunset on August 27 in honor of Neil's passing. On September 13, a memorial service was held in Washington National Cathedral. Many of Neil's friends and colleagues spoke movingly about their memories of the man. One of Neil's favorite singers, Diana Krall, sang "Fly Me to the Moon." The following day, with the whole Armstrong family in attendance, Neil's remains were scattered in the Atlantic Ocean as US Navy guns fired in his honor.

Neil's memory lives on in the form of the Armstrong Air and Space Museum in Wapakoneta, which opened in 1972.

CONCLUSION
INSPIRING OTHERS

Neil Armstrong will always be remembered for being the first human on the moon, but his life has served as an inspiration for other reasons, too. Many people have been impressed by his epic courage, his quiet humility, and his willingness to risk his life time and again in the name of human progress.

⋛ SPACE PIONEER ⋚

Neil and his contemporaries inspired new generations of astronauts and aerospace engineers to build on their achievements. As a result, we are living today in a world of:

→ permanently crewed space stations in Earth orbit
→ probes being sent to investigate planets, dwarf planets, moons, asteroids, and comets
→ robotic rovers exploring the surface of Mars

Now we possibly stand on the threshold of a new, exciting era of human-piloted space missions. There are plans to return to the moon and possibly establish a base there, and maybe even launch a crewed mission to Mars. Without intrepid pioneers like Neil Armstrong in the early days of spaceflight, none of this would have happened.

It's easy to forget how dangerous space travel was in the 1960s, with the technology available. The computers controlling *Apollo 11* had less processing power than a modern mobile phone. Yet, despite this, scientists and engineers of that time managed to land humans on the moon—a feat that will not be surpassed until a crewed mission to Mars takes place. You could say the *Apollo 11* crew was decades ahead of its time.

⋛ WHAT IF? ⋚

During the Mercury, Gemini, and Apollo programs, NASA and its small band of astronauts never wavered in their commitment to their work, despite many setbacks. The same is also true of the early cosmonauts of the Soviet Union. We have these brave men and women to thank for the progress we've made in space exploration since then. After the near disaster of Gemini 8 and the tragedy of Apollo 1, people like Neil could easily have said, "That's it—I'm done with space travel. It's too dangerous. I'm going to stick to flying airplanes instead."

What would have happened if those astronauts had said they weren't going to risk their lives anymore? They may have attracted some sympathy. At the time, many politicians and members of the public were opposed to the space program. It was hugely expensive and they simply couldn't see the point of it. Some even thought the idea of putting a human on the moon was impossible.

If the space program had been canceled, how would that have changed history? Well, for one thing, much of the technology we take for granted today simply wouldn't exist. For example, we wouldn't have:

→ communication satellites, which give us instantaneous worldwide communication via the internet and cell phones
→ weather satellites, which help us predict floods and storms, potentially saving millions of lives
→ the global positioning satellite (GPS) network, which allows ships, planes, cars, and people to find their way around

The space program has expanded our knowledge of astronomy and physics. Orbiting space telescopes such as Hubble enable astronomers to observe the universe clearly, without the distortions of the atmosphere, teaching us a great deal about the nature and origins of the solar system, the galaxy, and the universe.

The space program also brought us some unexpected benefits. The scientists and engineers who built spacecraft came up with all kinds of innovations that have transformed our lives, including:

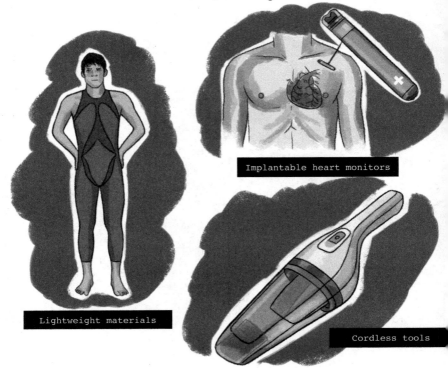

Lightweight materials

Implantable heart monitors

Cordless tools

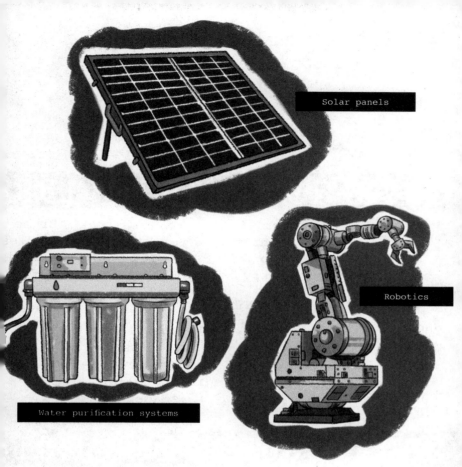

Solar panels

Water purification systems

Robotics

It has always been a part of human nature to want to explore the unknown and push at the boundaries of scientific knowledge. Space exploration allows us to do this. Much as our ancestors must have marveled at tales of new lands across the oceans, today we look on with curiosity, wonder, and awe as, decade by decade, probes explore ever deeper into the solar system and beyond.

Timeline of Space Firsts

1973 — *Pioneer 10* is the first probe to fly by Jupiter.

1974 — *Mariner 10* is the first probe to fly by Mercury.

1976 — The Viking landers take the first photos and soil samples from the surface of Mars.

1984 — Bruce McCandless performs the first untethered spacewalk.

2001 — *NEAR Shoemaker* makes the first landing on an asteroid (433 Eros).

2005 — *Cassini-Huygens* makes the first soft landing on Saturn's moon Titan.

2012 — *Voyager 1* is the first probe to reach interstellar space.

2014 — *Rosetta* makes the first soft landing on a comet.

Mir becomes the first long-term, consistently inhabited space station.

Galileo drops the first probe into the atmosphere of Jupiter.

1986   1990   1995   1997

Voyager 1 takes the first photograph of the whole solar system.

Mars Pathfinder rover Sojourner is the first rover on another planet (Mars).

The first space-grown food (lettuce) is eaten aboard the International Space Station.

New Horizons makes the first visit to Pluto.

2015

And in the future, who knows what benefits space exploration might bring? We might have space tourists and, eventually, vast orbiting cities where we could live and grow food. We could mine planets, moons, and asteroids for valuable minerals. Maybe one day, we could colonize Mars and become a two-planet species. This potential future wouldn't have been available to us if Neil and the other early astronauts hadn't blazed a trail.

SPACESHIP EARTH

When astronaut Bill Anders snapped his famous "Earthrise" photo from the window of *Apollo 8* in 1968, he had no idea of the impact it would have. People around the world were able to look at Earth for the first time as a small, vulnerable, beautiful planet in a vast universe, and therefore in need of protection. The photograph became one of the inspirations for the modern environmental movement.

Neil Armstrong hoped that the main legacy of the moon landing would be to teach us that we need to protect Earth.

Timeline

August 5
Neil Armstrong is born.

August 27
The Heinkel He 178, the first jet aircraft, makes its first flight.

World War I begins

1930   1932   1939

May 20
Amelia Earhart is the first woman to fly solo, nonstop, across the Atlantic.

The Cold War begins.

June 25
The Korean War begins.

1947   1950   1953

October 14
Charles "Chuck" Yeager pilots the first aircraft to break the sound barrier.

July 27
The Korean armistice is signed.

December 7
The Japanese attack on Pearl Harbor causes the United States to enter into World War II.

September 2
World War II ends.

1941   1944   1945   1946

June 20
A V-2 rocket becomes the first human-made object to reach space.

August
Neil Armstrong earns a student pilot's license and makes his first solo flight.

October 4
The Soviets launch Sputnik 1, the first artificial satellite.

September
Neil Armstrong is selected to be an astronaut for Project Gemini.

1957   1961   1962   1963

April 12
Soviet cosmonaut Yuri Gagarin makes the first human spaceflight.

November 22
President John F. Kennedy is assassinated.

March 16
Gemini 8 achieves world's first docking of two spacecraft in orbit.

July 20
Neil Armstrong and Buzz Aldrin land the lunar module *Eagle* on the moon's surface. Neil becomes the first human to set foot on the moon.

1966 1967   1969   197

January 27
Gus Grissom, Ed White, and Roger Chaffee are killed in a spacecraft fire during a rehearsal for the launch of *Apollo 1*.

April 1
The Sovie launch th first spa station, Salyut 1

January 28
The space shuttle *Challenger* explodes after launch, killing all seven crew members.

January 9
Astronomers find the first planets circling stars beyond our solar system.

1986   1991   1992

December 25
The Soviet Union is dissolved.

February 1
The Cold War officially ends.

2012

August 25
Neil Armstrong dies.

Further Reading

→ *The Apollo 11 Moon Landing: July 20, 1969* (24-Hour History) by Nel Yomtov (Heinemann Educational Books, 2014)

→ *The Apollo Missions* (Focus Readers: Destination Space: Voyager Level) by Patti Richards (Flux, 2018)

→ *Destination Moon: The Remarkable and Improbable Voyage of Apollo 11* by Richard Maurer (Roaring Brook Press, 2019)

→ *Neil Armstrong* (Raintree Perspectives: Science Biographies) by Catherine Chambers (Raintree, 2014)

Websites

→ bbc.com/bitesize/articles/zhx4k2p
Information about Neil Armstrong, including video clips and a quiz.

→ nasa.gov/mission_pages/apollo/missions/apollo11.html
A NASA website all about Apollo 11. It includes image and video galleries, story archives, and other information.

Glossary

aerodynamics: The study of moving air and how it interacts with solid bodies moving through it.

aileron: A hinged surface on the trailing edge of an aircraft's wing, used to control the aircraft's roll.

air-launch: A method of launching rockets from another aircraft in flight.

armistice: An agreement made by opposing sides in a war to stop fighting for a certain time.

artificial satellite: A human-made machine placed in orbit around Earth.

cornet: A brass instrument similar to a trumpet.

dogfighting: Close combat between military aircraft.

Earth orbit: An object's path around Earth.

Glossary

elevator: A hinged flap on the tail of an aircraft, used to control the pitch (upward or downward angle) of the aircraft's nose.

jettison: To drop or discard from a spacecraft, aircraft, or ship.

lunar module: A small craft used for traveling between the moon's surface and an orbiting spacecraft.

microgravity: Very weak gravity, as experienced in an orbiting spacecraft.

micrometeorites: Tiny particles in space.

nuclear warhead: The tip of a missile, which uses nuclear energy to cause a devastating explosion.

quarantine: A place of isolation in which people who may have been exposed to infectious diseases are kept for a certain period.

Glossary

radar: A system for detecting the presence, direction, distance, and speed of objects. It works by sending out pulses of radio waves, which are reflected off the object and back to the source.

radiation: The emission of energy in the form of high-energy subatomic particles. In high doses, radiation can harm living things.

reconnaissance: The military observation of a region to locate enemy positions.

simulator: A machine designed to provide a realistic imitation of the controls and operation of a vehicle such as a spacecraft. It is used for training purposes.

speed of sound: The speed traveled by a sound wave through a gas such as air. At room temperature (70° F, or 22.2° C), sound travels in air at a speed of 1,129 feet (344 m) per second.

Glossary

stall (of an aircraft): To stop flying and begin to fall because the speed is too low to maintain adequate lift.

strafe: To attack enemy positions on the ground with bombs or machine-gun fire from a low-flying aircraft.

thruster: A small rocket engine on a spacecraft used to make alterations in its flight path.

tumor: A swelling of a part of the body caused by an abnormal growth of tissue.

turbofan engine: A jet engine that contains a turbine-driven fan to provide additional thrust.

yaw (of an aircraft): Side-to-side movement.

Index

A

aerobatics, 46
aeronautical engineering, 36, 41–42, 70
ailerons, 38, 59, 74, 79
airplanes
  Aeronca Champion, 37, 40, 112
  B-29 Superfortress, 70–73, 78
  Grumman F8F-1 Bearcat, 47–48, 51
  Grumman F9F Panther, 51, 53–54, 57–59, 63
  model, 17, 23, 25, 31, 42–43, 52
  North American SNJ, 45–46
  Spirit of St. Louis, 19
  "Tin Goose," 15–16
  Wright Flyer, 14, 105
  X-15, 76–82, 112
Alcock, John, 20, 70
Aldrin, Buzz, 97, 101–102, 109, 111, 114–115, 117–118, 122–124, 126, 129, 137, 154
Anders, William, 11, 100, 119, 148
Apollo program
  Apollo 1, 10, 100, 142, 154
  Apollo 8, 11, 100, 148
  Apollo 10, 11
  Apollo 11, 2, 11, 100, 101–103, 105–111, 128–132, 141
Armstrong, Dean, 15, 28, 39, 40, 69, 88
Armstrong, Janet "Jan," 68–69, 74–75, 88, 119, 133, 136
Armstrong, June, 15, 18, 28, 48, 69
Armstrong, Stephen, 15–16, 40, 86
Armstrong, Viola, 15, 20, 28, 40, 48, 86, 120
astronauts, 2–3, 8–12, 26, 83–128, 132–133, 140–143, 146, 148–149, 152–155
  deaths of, 10, 104, 134
  selection process for, 83–85
atmosphere, 44, 77–81, 104, 144

Index

B

baritone horn, 28, 34, 42, 68
Blackford, John "Bud," 22, 24–25, 27–30
Blériot, Louis, 20
bombing, 46, 54, 57–58, 65, 70–71, 74
Borman, Frank, 11, 100
Boy Scouts, 24–27, 32, 40
Brown, Arthur, 20, 70

C

Cape Kennedy, 88, 103
centrifuge, 87, 90
Chaffee, Roger, 10, 154
Challenger, 104, 134, 155
Cold War, 4, 55, 152, 155
college, 41–43, 67–68
Collins, Michael "Mike," 101–103, 106–111, 124, 129, 137
Columbia (Apollo 11 command module), 102, 107–111, 117, 124, 127
Columbia (space shuttle), 104
cosmonauts, 6–7, 132, 142, 153
craters, 116–117

D

Day, Dick, 85
Dayton, 13–14

E

Eagle, 102, 107–125, 127–128, 154
Earhart, Amelia, 20, 70, 152
"Earthrise," 11, 148
Edwards Air Force Base, 70, 76, 80, 82, 85
extra-vehicular activity (EVA), 84, 88, 94, 101, 120, 123

F

flight
  around-the-world, 20, 134
  first ever, 14
  Neil Armstrong's first solo, 39
  transatlantic, 19–20, 85, 152
flying lessons, 36–40

G

Gagarin, Yuri, 7, 153
Gatty, Harold, 20
g-force, 87, 90

Index

Girl Scouts, 26
gravity, 87, 90, 96, 100, 106
   microgravity, 87
Grissom, Gus, 10, 154

H
high school, 32–34
Hubble Space Telescope, 144

I
illness, 74–75, 136

J
Juniper Hills, 69, 75

K
Kennedy, John F., 8, 153
Knudegard, Aubrey, 37, 39
Korean War, 54–67, 101, 152

L
Laika, 5
landings
   carrier, 46–48, 51–53,
     56, 59
   emergency, 62, 74, 82

Lindbergh, Charles, 19, 70,
   85, 133
Lovell, James, 11, 100
lunar landing, 2–3, 8–9, 12,
   95–98, 100–130
   timeline of, 106, 127

M
medals, 66, 94, 133
military service, 44–66
missiles, 4, 159
Mississippi Moonshiners,
   34–35
Mission Control, 92–93, 115,
   118, 126
moon
   far side of, 11
moonwalk, 122–124
   first words during, 12, 121
music, 28, 34–35, 68, 131

N
NASA (National Aeronautics
   and Space Administration),
   6, 8, 10, 83, 85–88, 94–96,
   124, 133, 137, 142, 157

Index

navy, 41–42, 44–66
Nixon, Richard, 123, 126–127, 130

O

Obama, Barack, 137–138
orbit, 4–5, 9, 11, 83–85, 90, 94–95, 100, 106, 113, 127, 132, 140, 144, 147, 149, 154, 158–159

P

Pearl Harbor, 24, 54, 153
pilot
  fighter, 45–66
  test, 70–74, 76–82
pilot's license, 39, 153
Port Koneta Airport, 36
Post, Wiley, 20
Project Gemini, 8, 83–84, 88–95, 101, 112, 142, 153–154
Project Mercury, 8, 83, 85, 142, 146
Purdue University, 42–44, 67–68, 70, 131

R

re-entry, 93–94, 104
rockets, 4, 9, 72–73, 76–80, 88, 90, 95–97, 104, 106, 113, 134, 158, 161
rocket scientists, 4
rocks, 116–117

S

satellites, 4–6, 143, 153, 158
  Explorer 1, 6
  Sputnik 1, 5, 153
  Sputnik 2, 5
  Vanguard, 5
Saturn, 146
Saturn V, 9, 95, 106–107
science fair, 29–30
Sea of Tranquility, 114–115
Shearon, Janet, see Armstrong, Janet
Shepard, Alan, 8
Solacoff, Konstantin "Kotcho," 22, 24–25, 27, 29–30, 136
Soviet Union, 4–7, 55, 132, 142, 153–155
space
  eating in, 90, 108–109

Index

    first American in, 8
    first man in, 7, 153
    first woman in, 7
    sleeping in, 109
Space Race, 4, 8, 132
space station, 140, 147, 154
spacesuits, 2, 9, 84

T

Tereshkova, Valentina, 7
timelines, 106, 127, 146–147, 152–155
training
    to become an astronaut, 87
    for the lunar landing, 96–99, 102
    naval, 44–54
Tranquility Base, 118, 131

U

Upper Sandusky, 22–24, 31, 136

V

Venera, 7
Venus, 7

W

Wapakoneta, 31, 36, 112, 131
White, Ed, 10, 88, 154
Wolf Patrol, 22–25, 27
World War II, 4, 45, 70, 152–153
Wright, Orville, 13–14, 105, 133
Wright, Wilbur, 13–14, 105, 133

FOLLOW THE TRAIL!

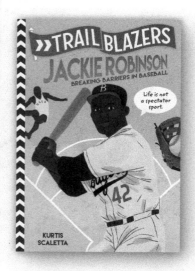

TURN THE PAGE FOR A SNEAK PEEK AT THESE TRAILBLAZERS BIOGRAPHIES!

Excerpt text copyright © 2019 by Kurtis Scaletta.
Excerpt illustrations copyright © 2019 by Artful Doodlers.
Published in the United States by Random House Children's Books,
a division of Penguin Random House LLC, New York

TRAIL BLAZERS

JACKIE ROBINSON
BREAKING BARRIERS IN BASEBALL

Life is not a spectator sport.

KURTIS SCALETTA

Jackie at UCLA
1939-1941

→ **Football:** Jackie is called "the greatest ball carrier in the nation." In 1939, the Bruins go undefeated, though three games end in ties.

→ **Basketball:** Dazzling play by Jackie helps end a long losing streak by the Bruins but isn't enough to give them a winning season.

→ **Baseball:** Jackie once again plays short and gets a reputation for stealing bases but goes into a hitting slump he can't break out of.

→ **Track and Field:** Jackie sets a conference record and wins the NCAA title for the long jump.

→ **Combined:** Jackie is the first athlete at UCLA to "letter" in four sports—meaning he has significant playing time at the varsity level.

LOVE AND WAR

Jackie continued to shine in his second year at ULCA, but the football team and basketball team both had losing seasons. Something happened that was more important than sports or even his education. He met a student named Rachel Isum. Jackie was drawn to Rachel's intelligence and compassion.

At first, he later wrote, Jackie experienced a new kind of prejudice. Rachel Isum knew he was a star athlete and had seen him play. She was convinced he was cocky and full of himself. But as she got to know him, she learned Jackie had a serious mind and—more important—respected that she had one, too. After they'd known each other for a year, they were deeply in love.

No matter what happens, this relationship is going to be one of the most important parts of my life.

Jackie's appeal crossed color lines. Author Myron Uhlberg wrote of how his deaf father connected with Jackie because they were both out of place in the world. Bette Bao Lord wrote a fictionalized memoir called *In the Year of the Boar and Jackie Robinson*, about how Jackie's courage helped her overcome her own barriers as a Chinese immigrant. Anyone who had ever been told they didn't belong, or who stood out for their differences, felt a connection.

And some fans loved Jackie simply because he was an exciting player to watch. He would get on base, take a lead, and dare the pitcher to make a throw. He was always a threat to steal. He would steal third base with two outs. He would steal home! Some fans compared him to baseball's all-time greatest base runner, Ty Cobb. Jackie's fearlessness on the base path lifted the rest of the team. They hit better because the pitchers were rattled and infielders were distracted.

Memorabilia

- Buddy Johnson record, *"Did You See Jackie Robinson Hit That Ball?"*

- Collectible cards

- Cover of *Time* magazine

- Jackie Robinson comic book

Excerpt text copyright © 2019 by Anita Ganeri.
Excerpt illustrations copyright © 2019 by Artful Doodlers.
Published in the United States by Random House Children's Books,
a division of Penguin Random House LLC, New York.

»TRAIL BLAZERS
JANE GOODALL
A LIFE WITH CHIMPS

Every individual matters.

ANITA GANERI

≥ BEASTS AT THE BIRCHES ≤

Despite the war, Jane spent many happy years at the Birches. To her delight, the house had a large, rambling garden, where she played for hours on end. Jane's favorite tree was a big beech tree. She loved it so much that Danny gave it to her, officially, for her tenth birthday. Jane was often found perched on a branch of her tree, reading a book or doing her homework.

Jane also collected a large number of pets, including a tortoise called Johnny Walker, a slow worm called Solomon, a canary called Peter, not to mention several terrapins, guinea pigs, and cats. Jane and Judy also had their own "racing" snails with numbers painted on their shells. The girls kept the snails in a wooden box covered with a piece of glass and with no bottom, so that the snails could feed on fresh dandelion leaves as the girls moved the box around the lawn.

Animal Fact File

Name: Peter
Animal: Canary
Behavior: Slept in a cage but was free to fly around during the day.

≡ THE ALLIGATOR CLUB ≡

As well as watching the birds, squirrels, foxes, insects, and spiders that came into the garden, Jane started her own nature club. It was called the Alligator Club and had four members—Jane; Judy; and their two best friends, Sally and Sue Cary, who came to stay at the Birches during the summer breaks. Each girl had to choose an animal as her code name—Jane was Red Admiral, Sally was Puffin, Sue was Ladybird, and Judy was Trout.

Primate, Monkey, or Ape?

There are more than three hundred species of primates. They all share many features, including large brains compared to the size of their bodies, forward-facing eyes, and flexible limbs and hands for grasping. But, while monkeys and apes (chimps, bonobos, gorillas, orangutans, and gibbons) are both primates, monkeys are not the same as apes. Here's how to tell them apart:

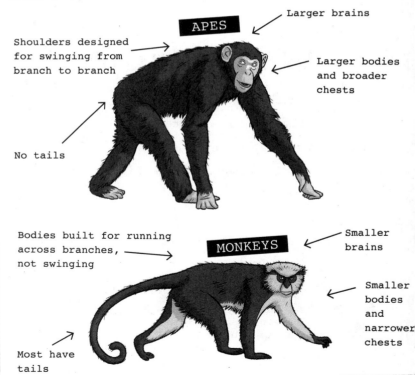

APES
- Larger brains
- Shoulders designed for swinging from branch to branch
- Larger bodies and broader chests
- No tails

MONKEYS
- Bodies built for running across branches, not swinging
- Smaller brains
- Smaller bodies and narrower chests
- Most have tails

Over the next few months, Jane's frustration grew. Sometimes, she didn't see any chimps for days, and when she did, she couldn't get close enough to observe them properly. So as not to startle the chimps, Jane wore clothes that blended in with the forest, and sat patiently for hours. The minute she tried to move nearer, the chimps scampered off. She was getting worried that if she didn't get results soon, Leakey would have to cancel the project, and she would have to leave Gombe.

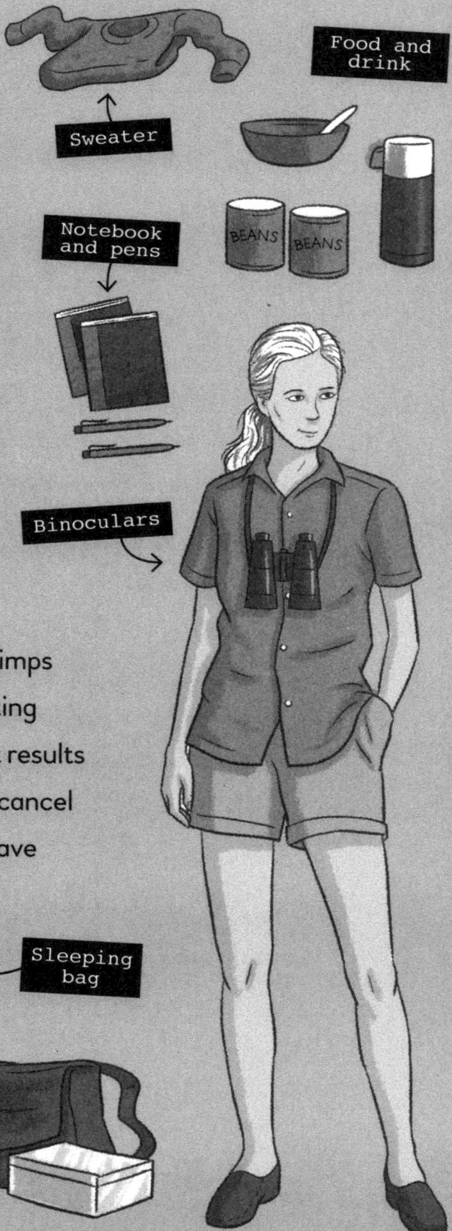

Sweater

Food and drink

Notebook and pens

Binoculars

Sleeping bag

Bagged lunch

Excerpt text copyright © 2019 by Sandra A. Agard.
Excerpt illustrations copyright © 2019 by Artful Doodlers.
Published in the United States by Random House Children's Books,
a division of Penguin Random House LLC, New York.

>>TRAIL BLAZERS
HARRIET TUBMAN
A JOURNEY TO FREEDOM

"I should fight for my liberty."

SANDRA A. AGARD

HARRIET'S ESCAPE

That night, Harriet went about her usual chores. John was hardly speaking to her these days, and they spent most evenings in silence. When she knew John was sound asleep, she got up quietly and helped herself to some ash cake (a type of bread), a piece of salt herring, and her wedding quilt.

Rather than set off into the woods, Harriet decided to head for Bucktown to the farm on the edge of the town. She was going to ask that white woman she had met by the road for assistance. It was a risky move—although the woman had said she'd help, Harriet couldn't know whether she'd really meant it, or how committed she would be to her offer once she discovered that Harriet was a runaway.

She uttered a quick prayer, walked toward the woman's door, and gently tapped on it. In the stillness of the night, the knock sounded so loud. The door opened, and the Quaker woman appeared. To Harriet's great relief, the woman nodded and asked Harriet to come in. She led Harriet into the kitchen and told her to sit down. She wrote two names on a piece of paper, then gave Harriet directions of where to go next.

The first stop, or station, on the Underground Railroad was another farm; Harriet couldn't miss it—there were two white posts with round knobs on them. The people there would give her food and clothing and keep her safe until it was time to move to the next place.

⇃ FAME AND FORTUNE ⇃

As she grew more famous, it became difficult for Harriet to make as many trips down South as before. Still desperate to help the Underground Railroad's efforts, in 1858 she began lecturing at locations all over the North. Her firsthand accounts of the Underground Railroad and its workings proved very popular, and she raised even more money to help fugitives, station masters, and conductors fighting to free slaves.

She was invited to speak in the parlor rooms of high society in Concord and Boston. In these anti-slavery speeches, Harriet told fascinating stories of her narrow escapes. Money poured in as more and more people heard about her amazing rescues.

⇃ HARRIET'S STORIES ⇃

One time, Harriet was traveling during the day in her home state of Maryland. She was wearing a large sunbonnet and kept her head bowed, but when she passed a former employer, Harriet worried that she would be recognized. Luckily, she'd just bought a couple of chickens at the market.

Thinking quickly, she opened the cage of chickens, which fluttered and squawked, causing an awful noise and diverting attention from herself.

On a different occasion, Harriet was traveling in a railway coach and noticed two gentlemen quietly discussing whether she was the woman on the Wanted poster at the station. Never one to panic, she simply picked up a newspaper and began to "read" it. Harriet Tubman was known to be illiterate—so this woman reading the paper studiously surely could not be the fugitive!

COMING SOON . . .

Albert Einstein

Beyoncé

Stephen Hawking

J. K. Rowling